SON OF A GUN

SON OF A GUN

JUSTIN ST. GERMAIN

Tuskar Rock Press
London

First published in the United States in 2013 by Random House, an imprint of The Random House Publishing Group, a division of Random House, Inc., New York.

First published in e-book in Great Britain in 2013 by Tuskar Rock Press, an imprint of Atlantic Books Ltd.

This trade paperback edition published in Great Britain in 2014 by Tuskar Rock Press.

10 9 8 7 6 5 4 3 2 1

A CIP catalogue record for this book is available from the British Library.

Trade paperback ISBN: 9781782390640
E-book ISBN: 9781782390657

Printed by ScandBook AB, Sweden 2013

Atlantic Books
An Imprint of Atlantic Books Ltd
Ormond House
26–27 Boswell Street
London
WC1N 3JZ

www.atlantic-books.co.uk

Book design by Christopher M. Zucker

For my mother

I was riding my bike home from class when a plane roared overhead, a green A-10 flying so low I could read its markings. I took my eyes off the road to watch it cross the sky. I'd been living in Tucson for a year, and hardly noticed the planes anymore as they flew over the city, to and from the air force base. But it had been nine days since the towers fell and we were all newly conscious of planes. I was twenty years old, and thought often of the future; I knew the world had changed, but I didn't know how much.

I rode my bike recklessly, helmetless and against traffic, hopping curbs and cutting across yards on my way to the rented house I shared with my brother, sweating through my shirt in the liquid heat. The streets shimmered like rivers. It was almost the end of summer, the last days of a long siege.

When I remember that bike ride, it's always beautiful: a bright expansive sky, tires whizzing on the road, my heart still whole and beating fast. About a mile, that ride, from the university mall gone brown and patchy after months of punishing sun, by the bricks and banners of Greek Row, down the sidewalks of strip malls along Speedway, past the squat stucco houses of my neighborhood, to the dirt yard of our bungalow, where, inside, the phone is ringing. A mile, a few minutes of my life, a few hundred beats of a young heart, but in my memory it lasts forever, and I remain that young man riding his bike, never reaching that front porch. That moment is golden, it's gone, it's a myth, but I remember it.

When I reached our driveway, I got off my bike to check the mailbox. The screen door flew open and my brother emerged, red faced and weeping, phone in hand, struggling to speak through the tears and mucus, his shrinking throat—but that struggle wasn't necessary, because I had never seen him anything like that before, so I knew what he was going to say. He let the screen door slam behind him. I dropped my bike in the yard. He bent at the waist and pinched the bridge of his nose with one hand, still holding the phone in the other. I hoped he'd never find his voice.

"She's dead."

"Who?" I had the sense of being watched, as if I would be expected to ask.

"Mom," he said. "Mom's dead." He turned and walked inside.

I crossed the yard, climbed the porch steps, and stood on the threshold. Josh walked around our living room, circling the couch. He told the person on the phone that he had to go and hung up.

"Who was that?"

"Connie." She and her husband, Bob, were our mother's best friends. "She was supposed to meet them for lunch and didn't. Bob went to the property and found her."

"What do you mean, *found* her?" The heat pressed against my back. I couldn't go inside until I made sense of this feeling: not shock, not grief—those would come later—but recognition, as if I had always known this moment would come.

"She got shot."

I

"What did you want?"
"Just to live a normal life."
"There is no normal life, Wyatt.
There's just life. Get on with it."
"Don't know how."

—DOC HOLLIDAY AND WYATT EARP,
Tombstone

THE BEAST

———

S oon after we learned that our mother was dead, my brother and I went to a bar. We'd already worked the phones. Josh had called our grandparents, who'd been divorced for forty years but both still lived in Philadelphia. Grandpop said he'd book the first flight he could, but air travel was snarled from the attacks nine days earlier. Grandma was afraid of flying, so she stayed in her rented room in suburban Philly, wrecked and helpless. I called my dad's house in New Hampshire, but he wasn't home. Eventually he called back. I told him she was dead and a long pause ensued, one in a litany of silences between my father and me, stretching across the years since he'd left and the distance between us, thousands of miles, most of America. Finally he said she was a good person, that he'd always cared for her. He asked if I wanted him to fly to Arizona. I said he didn't have to and hung up.

I emailed my professors and told them what had happened, that I wouldn't be back in class for a while. I called the office of the college newspaper where I worked and told my boss. Josh called in sick to his bartending job. Then we sat on the couch with our roommate, Joe, an old friend from Tombstone we'd known since grade school. It was a Thursday, and we had nothing to do. Somebody suggested the French Quarter, a Cajun joint nearby that had spicy gumbo and potent hurricanes. It seemed like a good idea: I'd heard stories of grief in which the stricken couldn't eat, but I was hungry, and I needed a drink. So that's where we spent our first night without her.

When we walked in, President Bush was on TV, about to give a speech. The jukebox was turned off, as it had been since the attacks, because now everybody wanted to hear the news. Joe went to the bar to talk to some of the regulars. Josh and I took a booth in the corner. Orion, the bartender and a friend of ours, came over and told us he was sorry, and to have whatever we wanted on the house. I wondered if Joe had just told him or if he'd already heard. I didn't know yet how quickly or how far the news would travel, that within a few hours we wouldn't need to tell anyone about our mother, because everyone would already know.

I flipped through the menu but couldn't understand it. We'd both put our cell phones on the tabletop, and mine rang, chirping as it skittered across the glass. I ignored it.

"What now?" I asked.

Josh kept his eyes on the menu and shook his head. "There's not much we can do."

"Should we go out there?" I didn't know what to call the place where she'd died; it wasn't home, because we'd never lived there, and it didn't have a name. It was just a piece of land in the desert outside of Tombstone.

"We can't. The property is a crime scene."

I asked him if we should talk to the cops and he said he already had, that we were meeting with them on Monday. I asked about a funeral home and he said the coroner had to do an autopsy first, the cops said it was standard procedure. There was a long pause. My mother and her parents always said Josh was more like my father, difficult to read, and he looked like Dad, too, sharp nosed and handsome. I got more from my mother, they said, the dark and heavy brows, the temper, the heart on my sleeve. But if I was like my mother, why was I so numb?

Food arrived. Through the windows I watched the sky outside go purple and the traffic on Grant die down. A hot breeze blew through the open door. On television, President Bush identified the enemy, a vast network of terror that wanted to kill all of us, and finally he said the name of a murderer.

"Do you think Ray did it?" I asked. The police couldn't find our stepfather or the pickup truck he and my mother owned. He was the only suspect, but I didn't want to believe it.

Josh waited awhile to respond, chewing, letting his eyes wander the walls decorated with beads and Mardi Gras masks and a neon sign above the bar that said "Geaux Tigers."

"We'll know for sure when they find him."

A pool cue cracked and a ball fell into a pocket with a hollow knock. My phone rang again. I didn't answer. My voice mail was already full, and the calls kept coming, from distant family, my friends, her friends, acquaintances from Tombstone, people I hardly knew. At first I'd answered, but the conversations went exactly the same: they'd say they were sorry and I'd thank them for calling; they'd ask for news and I'd say there wasn't any; they'd ask if there was anything they could do and I'd say no. It was easier to let them leave a message.

On the TV, the president talked about a long campaign to come, unlike anything we'd ever seen. He said to live our lives and hug our children. He said to be calm and resolute in the face of a continuing threat.

"You think he'd come here?" I asked. Ray knew where we lived. He'd been to the house a few times, with our mother, staying on the pullout couch in the living room.

"The detective mentioned that. He said he doubted it, but to keep an eye out."

I wondered what good that would do but didn't ask. Josh said we'd know more on Monday, after we met with the cops.

"What do we do until then?"

I could tell Josh was wondering the same thing: what the hell were we going to *do*? "Wait, I guess."

Behind me the pool table rumbled as the players began another game. I looked down at my plate, realized that my food was gone, and scanned the old newspaper articles from New Orleans pasted beneath the glass tabletop. My mother was dead. I leaned back against the vinyl seat and finished my beer, watching the president try to soothe a wounded nation. He said that life would return to normal, that grief recedes with time and grace, but that we would always remember, that we'd carry memories of a face and a voice gone forever.

Late that night, I said a prayer for the first time in months. When I was a kid, Mom had always made me say prayers before bed, and it became a habit, something I felt guilty about if I didn't do. I'd stopped praying regularly after I left home, but that night I prayed for my mother's soul, because I knew she'd want me to, and I figured it couldn't hurt.

I didn't pray for my own safety; I knew better than to rely on God for that. Instead, I got up off my knees, pulled a long gray case out of my closet, laid it on the bed, and flipped the catches. Inside, on a bed of dimpled foam, lay a rifle, a gift from my father on my thirteenth birthday, an old Lee-Enfield bolt-action. I lifted it out of the case, loaded it, chambered a round, and rested it against the wall by my bed. Then I tried to sleep, but every time a car passed, I sat up to peek out the window, expecting to see Ray in our front yard.

After a few sleepless hours I got up and went to my desk. I turned on my computer, opened a Word document, and stared at the blank screen. I kept a journal, in which I wrote to the future self I imagined, chronicling important moments in my life, because I thought he might want to remember, and because it made me feel less alone. I would write about how much I missed Tombstone, how dislocated I felt after moving from a town of fifteen hundred people to a city thirty times that size, how I felt like an impostor at school, was failing half my classes, would never graduate. I wrote about girls. I wrote about money, how little I had, my mounting debt, my fear that I wouldn't be able to cover tuition and rent. And I wrote about Mom, how she'd gone crazy after I moved out, how she and Ray had sold our trailer outside of Tombstone and gone touring the country with their horses, camping in national parks, how one day I'd get a card in the mail postmarked from Utah, and the next she'd send an email from Nebraska—all of them signed *xoxo, Mom and Ray*—and how she'd leave rambling messages on our answering machine at five o'clock in the morning, saying how much she loved and missed us.

I thought I should write something about that day, so the future me never forgot how it had felt to be twenty and motherless, my life possibly in danger, numb from shock and hating my own inability to feel. But I didn't know what to say. I was afraid I wouldn't be able to do the feeling justice, that I'd choose the wrong words. I was in my first literature class at the time, an American lit survey, and I'd just written a paper on Henry James's "The Beast in the Jungle." So I did what any English major would: I quoted someone else.

———

My mother is dead. The Beast has sprung.

It worked. I sat down to write at the end of every day for the next few weeks, and each time the words came easily. Sometimes I return to those entries, when I'm afraid I've begun to forget. But I can't read them for long without wanting to write back to my old self, to warn him of what's to come, to tell him that the Beast will always be with us.

I woke up the first day after learning of her death and turned off my alarm, then went back to sleep until the room got too bright. When I woke again, I looked out the window at the yard full of weeds. I stood, stretched, brushed my teeth. Walking down the hall into the living room, wondering what I'd do with the day ahead—it was Friday, so I had a softball game that night, and afterward somebody would be having a party—I glanced through the screen door at the front porch and remembered.

My grandfather arrived from Philly that afternoon, pale and harried, lighting new cigarettes with the still-burning stubs of the last. We went straight from the airport to a Denny's by the highway and sat drinking iced tea and watching cars pass by outside, planes taking off and landing, families piling out of minivans in the parking lot, other people going places. The world hadn't stopped, despite how it seemed to us.

When our food came, we picked at it and discussed our plans. My dad had decided to come and would be flying in the next day. On Monday we had meetings scheduled with the detectives and the funeral director and my mother's bank and lawyer, a gauntlet none of us wanted to think or talk about. My mother's closest friend, Connie, was taking care of the horses and Chance, Ray's dog, who'd been left behind. She said that my mother's property was still cordoned off, that the cops were there in a helicopter, looking for Ray or for his body. We'd go to Tombstone in the morning. For now, there was nothing we could do but try to get some rest.

Grandpop went to his hotel. Josh and I went home and sat on the couch watching pirated cable for the rest of the afternoon. As the room began to dim, I checked the time and remembered that I had a softball game in half an hour. I went to my room and changed. When I walked out carrying my bat bag, Josh asked where I was going.

"We've got a doubleheader."

"Seriously?"

I put on my hat and grabbed my keys off the coffee table. "There's nothing better to do."

"OK," he said, shrugging.

I realized it would be the first time we'd spent apart since we heard the news, and an unfamiliar feeling came over me: I was worried about him. "What are you going to do?"

"I might go to the Bay Horse."

The Bay Horse was a bar two blocks away where our roommate worked. I was glad to know Josh wouldn't be alone while I was gone, and the thought of joining them later at the Bay Horse gave me comfort. We spent a few nights a week in that smoky dive, playing darts and feeding the jukebox, writing graffiti in the bathroom, drinking ourselves into stupors.

I walked through the door and across the porch and out into the yard, where I stopped and looked back. The blinds were open, revealing my brother's face in the blue glow of the television. The house loomed gray below a purple sky; the stucco had cracked along the edge of the roof and one of the address numbers had been missing since I moved in. It was the only home I had left.

The dugout went quiet when I walked in. My teammates continued lacing their cleats, hanging bats in the racks, filling their mouths with sunflower seeds, but nobody spoke to me, and hardly a head turned in my direction. They were trying to act normal. They failed, but I appreciated the effort.

It was a coed league of born-again Christians. Our team's coach was a pastor. Most of the players, the men especially, took the games too seriously, heckling opponents and yelling at umpires, and nobody was any good. But I'd played ball my whole life and I missed being part of a team, so when my friend Brent had asked if I wanted to join, I'd jumped at the chance to play.

I spotted Brent at the far end of the metal bench and sat next to him. We'd known each other for a few years, had played together on our high school baseball team. I could tell that he had heard.

"You made it," he said.

I nodded. "Had to get away for a while."

"Sure." He worked a sunflower seed between his teeth, thinking of something to say, but just then the umps called us in for the pregame prayer. Before each game we stood in a circle around home plate and held hands while our coach, the pastor, said prayers that were clearly made up as he went. I was raised Catholic, communed and confirmed and all that, so it sounded like amateur hour to me, but I always went along, joined hands and bowed my head and pretended to listen.

That night's prayer was oppressive. I stood staring down at the dusty home plate, with my hat beneath my arm and a stranger's sweaty palm pressed against mine, listening to an error-prone second baseman preach about our great and just and loving God. At the end he said something about those of us suffering hard times and I wondered if he knew.

When it was over, I grabbed my glove. I played left and

liked ranging the outfield. The bats would ping and I'd be off, tracking down a deep fly ball at the fence, snaring a liner to the gap, trying to throw out runners at home. For a moment I'd forget that it was a coed church league, that the person I'd just robbed of a double was somebody's aunt. I'd forget the score, the number of outs. I'd forget about school and work, forget my name, forget who I was. The world shrank down to a field of grass, and all I had to do was catch the ball.

I played well that night. I made a basket catch on a liner over my head, slid to pluck a Texas leaguer just before it hit the grass. I don't remember what I did at the plate, only sprinting across the outfield, catching everything. A lull would come, a few groundouts in a row, a string of walks, and I'd feel something stalking me just outside the white ring of the field lights, something creeping in. But then the yellow ball would rocket across the night sky and I'd be off, gauging its depth, fixing on a point ahead and running, running as fast as I could.

HER SAVIOR

My mother loved to tell the story of how Ray had saved her. She met her fifth and final husband by calling the police. I wasn't there, but I heard her tell the story over and over, and it grew more dramatic every time. She was managing a Mexican restaurant in Tombstone, Arizona, the small and legendary town where I grew up, when one day a tourist, a big and angry man, started harassing her about his bill. He said his tab was wrong. She said it was right. He called her a name. She told him to pay his bill and leave. He grabbed her arm. She pulled away, ran to the back room, and called the cops. The marshal's office was across the street, next to the O.K. Corral, and Ray showed up in a few minutes. He wrestled the man to the ground, cuffed him, dragged him outside to his police cruiser, and threw him in back. Then he came inside and asked my mother her name.

"My hero," Mom would say, only half joking. "It was love at first sight." She'd look over at him all dewy eyed, and he'd

---

blush and give a sheepish grin. The story never made much sense to me. A customer grabs her, and none of the employees intervene, not even Adonis, the hulking Greek waiter? How did the man get close enough to grab her in the first place if she was behind the bar? If the customer was so big and so mad, how did Ray, at five nine and a buck fifty, bring him down so easy? And why would Mom—a single mother of two boys, a former army paratrooper, the toughest woman I've ever known—have been afraid enough to call the cops? The mother I knew would have grabbed the order spike off the counter and stabbed that son of a bitch. She didn't take any shit from men unless she was in love with them.

But that was the story they stuck with.

I didn't meet Ray until a few weeks later. He'd started hanging around the restaurant, eating lunch with other cops. They'd all sit around a table stroking their mustaches and eating free chips and salsa. I'd never had any run-ins with Ray before, but I hated Tombstone cops, thought they were a bunch of power-tripping dicks. When they weren't busy harassing my friends and me for imaginary moving violations, trying to catch us driving drunk or riding dirty, the deputies would hang out in the parking lot of the Circle K, chatting up high school girls. Now they took their lunches at the restaurant, with my mother stopping every five minutes to refill their iced teas.

I had recently graduated from Tombstone High School and was living with Mom in a trailer outside of town. Josh had left for college a few years earlier, and she hadn't been dating any-one for a while before Ray, so I was used to being the man of the house. I worked as a line cook at a tourist steakhouse and was failing a couple of classes at the junior college in Sierra Vista. After work I'd drive my pickup truck out to the desert and drink cheap beer by the case with my friends from high school while we hatched elaborate plans for escape. Broke, single, getting fat, drunk, seventeen: I was white trash. I'd stop by my mother's restaurant to get free tacos. Now Ray was always there. Mom had mentioned him, but I didn't take it seriously until I saw the way his eyes followed her, the nervous gestures she made with her hands when she talked to him, the big smile every time he walked in the door. I'd seen it happen enough; I'd had three stepdads by then, and dealt with another dozen of her boyfriends at one time or another. I knew what was coming. But that didn't mean I had to like it.

Soon Ray started coming to the restaurant alone. She'd linger at his table, ignoring other customers, claiming she was on break. Mom didn't introduce us, and I wasn't about to make the effort. They'd talk in low voices, laughing too much, and I'd sit at another table, scarfing pollo asado, wondering how long this one would last.

At home I made cracks about Mom's bodyguard and asked if the restaurant had started serving doughnuts. She'd blush and change the subject. After a few weeks, she ambushed me one afternoon on the restaurant's patio, said she wanted me to meet someone, and walked me over to his table, where he sat reclining in the plastic chair with one arm resting on top of his holster, the other hand hooked in his belt. He was about ten years younger than my mother, in his early thirties. Judging by the cowboy hat on his knee and the shiny badge and the bushy mustache, I could tell he was trying to look like his famous predecessor, Wyatt Earp, whose face was plastered all over every gift shop in town. It wasn't working. Wyatt was tall and imposing, with a full head of hair and piercing eyes; Ray was runty and balding and had a bland, boyish face. We shook hands and I sat down. Mom did most of the talking. "Ray used to be a cop in Huachuca City," she said, like that was an accomplishment. When I didn't respond, she said, "Justin has friends there."

I did have friends there, potheads and delinquents who drag-raced and built homemade firearms. He'd probably arrested some of them.

"I like Tombstone better," Ray said.

"Me, too, I guess."

There was an awkward silence, then he put his hand on her knee. I said I had to go, kissed my mother on the cheek, told Ray I'd see him around. He said it was nice to meet me, but he was looking at her when he said it.

A few days later I came home from work and found him sitting at our dinner table. Mom asked if I was hungry. I wasn't hungry enough to sit there and watch them feed each other ice cream, so I went to my room. Later I heard their footsteps down the hall, the bass of his voice, her bedroom door closing.

My mother always had shitty taste in men. My father, who likes to point out that he was born in the same hospital as the lead singer of Grand Funk Railroad, is every bit the American man, the second son of an autoworker who joined the army at seventeen and got married and had two kids and got discharged and got divorced and didn't pay his child support. Now he's remarried, has two stepkids and two real kids he doesn't see enough, wishes things were different but doesn't do much about it, owns a ranch house at the edge of a midsized city with a truck and an old Corvette and a fishing boat in the garage, a lot of guns in a case in the basement, and spends most of his time working a blue-collar job, watching television, and drinking the nights away. He's my father by name and blood, but not by role: he left when I was two.

The next man my mother married was a car salesman in

North Carolina. Their marriage lasted only a couple of years, and I hardly remember him. After that she dated another army man, the jumpmaster of her airborne unit, and we all moved out to Arizona and they got engaged, but it fell apart when she met her third husband, a rich tourist visiting Tombstone whom she married for six months.

Then there was her fourth husband, Max, the only one I would really call a stepdad, because I hated him with all my heart, and he wished I didn't exist. Max was a burly red-faced Canadian, an alpha-male blowhard, full of threats and bluster and lies. He was the first man I ever saw abuse her, and then bring her back again and again by crying and pleading and claiming a chemical imbalance in his brain, until I thought she'd never leave him. When she finally did, I hoped she had wised up.

Before she met Ray, it seemed like Mom's taste in men was improving. She stopped getting married for a few years between Max and Ray, and she dated a pediatrician for a while, a pompous loudmouth, but he was rich and he didn't beat her. Then she dated another army man, an officer, who taught me how to drive a stick shift, because my mother didn't have the patience—every time she tried, we wound up stalled at a stop sign, screaming at each other. The officer would take me out on long drives in his Kia, which was so new it still had that smell, and as I ground the gears and spun the tires, he'd talk about my mother, how she didn't love him like he loved her, and I would listen, and feel bad, and sometimes give advice. But I never told him the one thing I had begun to fear was true: that if he wanted her to love him, he would have to hurt her. I came home from school one day and he was gone, the only trace of him a note left on my dresser that said: *Thank you for being my friend, Justin. Take care of Debbie.* Later she let it slip that he'd been married the whole time.

16

After that she dated Dave, the father of a friend of mine. Dave's son was also named Justin, and we were classmates in school. We moved into Dave's six-bedroom house on a hill outside of town, with an indoor pool and a hot tub and a TV that was five feet across, and it was awkward for a while, but soon I began to like Dave. Every day at breakfast, we'd exchange good mornings and he'd crack a couple of jokes, and then I wouldn't see him again until the next day. He never asked me about her exes, didn't try to threaten me or buy me off. For the first time in my life, I wanted her to get married. I was a senior in high school, almost on my own, and I hoped she'd find some stability before I left. They had their disagreements, shouting matches that spilled from their bedroom through the house and into the garage, where he'd kick a dent in her car and she'd peel off down the driveway, clipping the gatepost with her bumper, yelling out the window that I should pack my bags. But he always apologized, and he never hit her. Their relationship ended like hers always did, offstage, the decision already made by the time she told me we were moving out.

There were a few others somewhere along the way, men who hung around for weeks or months and then disappeared, men I never bothered to acknowledge, men whose names I don't remember. So when she introduced me to this drawling, dull-eyed cop with eagles tattooed on his forearms, I figured she'd get sick of him soon enough. The first time Ray stayed the night, I didn't speak to her for days. When she brought him home again anyway, I started to worry.

One morning there was a knock at my bedroom door. I opened it and saw Ray. "Got a minute?" he asked. By the way he looked me in the eye, I knew he'd been rehearsing. I glanced around my room for an excuse but couldn't find one, so I followed him out into the living room. He sat at one end of the long black sectional, a yard sale find of Mom's, which ran along the wall beneath a framed motivational poster of a horse rearing in front of a red sunset. A black rug with pink and teal triangles covered the carpet under a glass coffee table. I hated that room: by then the books and magazines I bought with my restaurant paychecks had suggested to me a world beyond mine, and I was starting to understand what white trash meant, that it meant us.

He sat at one end of the couch. I sat at the other and waited for him to begin. I'd been hoping we could skip this—her last few boyfriends hadn't bothered having one of these talks, and it worked better that way. Did he know how many man-to-mans I'd had, how many promises I'd heard? Would he start with how much he loved her? How he was different from the others? At least I was too old for the new-dad bit.

"I know you're mad," Ray said.

"You're right."

"I'd be mad, too."

I waited to see where he was heading. At least he wasn't playing the tough guy, not like some others had, with the line about how they were going to be there whether I liked it or not, so I'd better get used to it.

"I know how you feel. I've been in your shoes," he said. He told me about his family, that his parents had broken up when he was a kid, and when his mother brought a new man around, Ray had hated him at first. But that man had sat him down, just like this, and he'd said he wasn't going to hurt his mother, that she was safe with him. Ray decided to give him a chance, and sure enough, he realized he could learn a lot from the man who became his stepdad. Now he thought of him almost as a father. Ray finished the story and sat there looking satisfied, as if our chat were going just how he'd expected.

"Let's not get ahead of ourselves. You guys just met."

"That's true," he said. "But I like her, and she likes me."

"I've heard this before."

He said he knew there'd been other men, but he didn't care. He was no angel. And he liked the fact that Mom cared so much about her sons, that we were so close. "I'm not going to take her away from you," he said. We didn't have to be friends, but he hoped I'd give him a chance. And if I ever needed to talk, about the kind of things you can't mention to your mom, girls or drugs or trouble—things I'd always talked to my mother about—I could talk to him.

My instinct was to make a wiseass crack, walk away, and wait for her to leave him. But this was something new. He was treating me like a man, and that reminded me that I almost was: in a few months, I'd be eighteen, and even though I had no real plans, we both knew I'd be gone soon enough. He didn't have to bother with me. I'd been waiting him out; he could have done the same, and he would have won.

And I thought my mother needed someone. She'd had a hard time when my brother left for college, worried constantly, called too much. When I left, it would be even worse, because she'd be all alone, a fortysomething woman four times divorced managing a Mexican restaurant in Tombstone, living in a trailer. She'd seen worse and come through it; when she was twenty-five, my father left her with two young boys, no money, and a motorcycle, and she still managed to raise us, feed us, give us love. But I was trying to think like a man. I thought she needed someone to take care of her now, and as he sat there on the couch with his hands folded in his lap, looking me in the eye, I thought maybe Ray would do.

I started talking to Ray when he came around our place, and sitting with him at the restaurant. We talked about the things he knew: motorcycles, guns, the military. I learned a little bit about him. He'd been a marine, and had driven a truck in Desert Storm, but after the war he decided not to reenlist, became a cop instead. He started in Huachuca City and stayed for a few years, but got tired of the pay, so he moved to Tombstone, where he was getting tired of his boss. There were holes in his history, and he mentioned an ex-wife and kids whom he obviously didn't want to talk about. I could understand that; our family knew how to handle past lives.

When he moved in a few months later, I didn't make a scene. Ray didn't seem so bad anymore; in fact, I was starting to like him. He took over some of the tasks I hated most, feeding my mother's two horses, unloading hay bales, shoveling horseshit. He didn't say anything when I came home drunk, and sometimes when Mom wasn't there, we'd go out into the carport and he'd smoke his pipe and I'd smoke the cigarettes my mother threw away whenever she found them in my pockets. Ray knew a little bit about computers, and had brought an old one with him to our house, which he showed me how to use. When he discovered the sort of sites I'd been visiting, he didn't say a word, just cracked a crooked smile and showed me how to clear the history. He even tried to teach me how to play the guitar, but it was hopeless: I have fat fingers and a tin ear, and he only knew a few chords. Ray also brought his dog with him, Chance, a Rottweiler-chow mix. I felt the same way about the dog as I did about his owner: he seemed mellow but protective, and while we would probably never quite be friends, he was good to have around.

By the time I moved out, Ray and I got along fine. The day

I left, we stood out in the driveway, me and Mom and him, just past the shade of the carport awning, by the pickup truck she'd bought me when I turned sixteen, now loaded down with everything I owned worth taking, its springs sagging to the stops. It was around noon, midsummer, bright but not that hot at Tombstone's elevation, almost a mile high, the air clear, the city sharp and gleaming in the distance, the cypresses tall and green, tin rooftops glinting in the sun like shards of glass. The hills between our place and town were covered in scrub brush and barbed wire and trailers sitting crookedly in bull-dozed lots, front yards full of rusting cars. At the edge of our lot the horses nipped each other in the corrals, and the wind blew the smell of horseshit up to us. I knew this place, loved it, and wasn't sure I wanted to leave, but knew I had to. Everybody in town had been telling me that my whole life, even Mom, though she'd stopped saying it as this day got closer.

Chance spun around our feet, wagging his tail and whining. I figured I'd start with the dog. I bent down and scratched behind his ears, let him lick my hand. Then I stood and turned to my mother. She was playing with her hair, checking the tips of the long brown strands for split ends; she did that when she was nervous or upset. She was wearing sunglasses, the enormous plastic shades sold in drugstores to senior citizens, the ones I made fun of her for—she worried about her eyes, and about mine, told me to wear sunglasses all the time so I wouldn't get cataracts—and when she took them off, she was already starting to cry. I'd seen those eyes change in different lights and moods, almost black when she was angry or soft brown like this when she was sad, or when she was in love again, and I'd seen the skin around them wrinkle and spot in the eighteen years I'd known no life other than one with her. She was more than a foot shorter than me, so I had to reach way down to let her hug me, squeezing hard with her muscu-

lar arms. When the doctors had told her after my brother that another child would mean another C-section, she'd had me anyway, then hemorrhaged and had an emergency hysterectomy to save her life. After that she was scarred and barren, on hormone pills, prone to fractures—a shattered wrist, pins in her foot—and as she raised and loved and competed with men for the rest of her life, through motherhood and marriages, careers as a soldier and a small-business owner, she began to seem almost masculine, broad shoulders and a bracing grip, tough as rawhide.

She hugged me, holding on tight. I told her not to cry, that I wasn't going far, even as I looked over her shoulder toward the horizon. I think I told her that I loved her, but I'm not sure.

She let go, looked down, wiped the tears from her face, and forced a smile. Ray put one arm around her and extended the other to me. We shook hands. His grip was firm and I tried to match it. "Take care of her," I said, and he nodded, and it was like we were two cowboys selling a horse. Then I got in my truck and headed west, toward Tucson and college and the house where I would be living with my brother when the call came.

THE CRIME SCENE

———

We left early in two cars: Josh rode with Grandpop in his rental, and Joe rode with me in my truck, which we would need to haul anything of my mother's that we wanted to keep. We climbed the hill into Tombstone, passed the city limit sign, and drove straight through town on the highway without speaking, watching the landmarks slide by, the Best Western and Boothill and the Circle K, one of the houses we'd lived in, the marshal's office and the Mexican restaurant where Mom met Ray. The town felt hostile: I knew everyone would be talking about my mother's death, gossiping, twisting the truth.

At the far end of town we turned on Gleeson Road and took it until my truck rumbled across a cattle guard and the road turned to dirt. I drove slowly so Grandpop could follow. I was the only one of us who knew the way. I was the only one who'd been there.

———

About a year after I left home, my mother and Ray bought land in Gleeson, a dozen miles east of Tombstone. They said they wanted to be near Josh and me, but they also wanted to get away from Tombstone; as a former cop and a serial divorcée, they'd both made their share of enemies, and they were sick of the rumors that run rampant in a town that small and dull. Gleeson didn't make any sense—it was farther from where we lived than Tombstone was, and if they wanted to stay in the area, there were better places to live. They could have moved to Sierra Vista, which had movie theaters and grocery stores and chain restaurants and a new Target. Or, if they really wanted to be hippies, as they sometimes called themselves, they could have moved to Bisbee, an artsy tourist town by the border.

Instead they chose Gleeson, a busted copper camp way out in the desert. Even in its boom years, Gleeson had been an afterthought, smaller and poorer than Tombstone or Bisbee, and a century later it was less than that: a few closed-down mines, a jail in ruins, an abandoned post office, a graveyard full of crooked crosses, and a handful of recluses living in trailers. Nobody famous had ever lived or died or killed anyone in Gleeson, so when the mines shut down it became what Tombstone would have if it weren't for the Wyatt Earp legend: a real ghost town, one of hundreds rotting in the rural West, remote and dangerous—collapsing mine shafts, arsenic in the water—and mostly forgotten, with no utility service or telephone lines, no cops or fire department. Gleeson hardly even had tourists, who wisely decided not to venture too far from the chicken fingers and stagecoach tours of Tombstone.

I drove slowly down Gleeson Road, checking the rearview

every few minutes to make sure Grandpop's rental car was still there, following in a plume of dust. Just before Gleeson, I turned off the road onto a dim track and stopped at a metal gate. Tire tracks striped the dust: the crooked tread of the police SUVs, the dual rear wheels of an ambulance. Ray's trail must have been there, somewhere in the latticework of tracks, but this wasn't one of the cowboy stories I'd read as a kid: I wasn't going to hunt him down.

A strip of yellow police tape held the gate shut. I ripped it off and opened the gate, then stood for a moment looking at the land. Ahead, the road dipped and crossed a rocky wash, then climbed a low hill and split to form a loop around the buildings: a small barn with a corral, a shed, and an Airstream travel trailer. Mom and Ray had bought the trailer as a temporary place to live while they researched plans to build a rammed-earth house—another of their crackpot ideas—and it was where they'd lived together, with no running water and no air-conditioning, just a gas generator providing noisy and expensive electricity part of the time. Of all the homes she'd had, all the temporary places with temporary men, the worst was where she died.

Grandpop's rental car wouldn't make it down the driveway, so he and Josh got out and walked. I drove through the gate and paused before realizing there was no reason to close it behind us, then followed the trail across the wash and around the back of the trailer, where I parked by the barn. We met in the boot-trampled clearing between the buildings. Nobody spoke for a solid minute as we surveyed the scene. A lawn chair lay tipped over. The rocks of the fire pit had been scattered. The horse trailer sat empty with its tongue propped up on cinder blocks. The tin-roofed barn was still half full of hay. Dust swirled in the corrals, and at the edge of the clearing mesquite branches stirred in the breeze. It was a beautiful day, warm and clear, the sky cloudless and deep. I remembered that it was the equinox. Fall had come.

I'd only been to my mother's property once, during the previous spring, near the end of my first year in Tucson. The university had sent me a letter threatening to kick me out if my grades didn't improve. I was broke and in debt. One night, leaving my girlfriend's apartment after an argument, I backed my truck into a telephone pole in the parking lot and lost it, wound up curled on my bedroom floor, sobbing.

The next day was Good Friday. I woke up in the afternoon and felt the same, as if a dam had broken and I was drowning. So I did what I always did when I got into trouble: I called my mother. She didn't answer. Since she'd moved to Gleeson, she rarely answered: her cell phone couldn't get steady service out there. When I did get through, our conversations were full of static and often ended without warning when she lost the signal. I sat on my bedroom floor staring at the texturing on the ceiling, trying to find a pattern, wondering when she'd call me back, wondering what I would do if I didn't feel better soon.

My phone rang. It was Mom. She was in Tombstone running errands, so the signal was clear for once. She said she'd been in the feed store and had missed my call. When I told her how I felt, she said to drive down there, that she missed me and wanted me to see the place where they were living. She gave me directions, said she'd meet me at the entrance to the driveway.

I got in my dented truck and drove. When I reached Tombstone it was dusk. I went through town slowly, watching the setting of my childhood pass by; I was a sucker for Tombstone's false nostalgia, and missed it even though I remembered how badly I'd wanted to leave less than a year before. But already my hometown had begun to feel strange, and I didn't know if the town had changed or if I had.

By the time I made it to the cattle guard where Gleeson Road turned to dirt, the sky was fully dark. The scattered lights of Tombstone receded in my rearview until I crested a hill and they disappeared, the land rolling black to every horizon. I knew rural places, but this emptiness was something else: I was alone out here, like a pioneer or a survivor, the first man on a new planet or the last one on Earth. In the half hour it took to drive to Mom's property I didn't see another car, only shotgunned signs warning of road hazards. After the mile marker she had mentioned in her directions, I slowed down and watched the side of the road, but still she shocked me when I saw her, a wraith at the edge of my headlights, standing on the shoulder of the road and waving. I stopped and she walked out of the void into my yellow headlight beams. She got inside and hugged me and guided me the rest of the way.

In their claustrophobic trailer we sat in the light of a lantern and the three of us had a long talk. I was there to see her, but there was nowhere for Ray to go, pitch dark outside and cold as it was. I told her I couldn't make sense of anything, that I was afraid of something I couldn't name. A panic attack, she said; she'd had them during hard times in her life, before giving birth and after Dad left, during airborne school and her divorces. Ray claimed to have known something similar in boot camp and at the police academy, but I didn't know if he was telling the truth or if he was just trying to be part of the family. Mom told me the way to deal with times like these was to focus on the present and not to think about what's still to come. Soon it will pass. It always does. After talking to her, I felt lightened and relieved, calm for the first time in days. When I left that place out in the desert, it seemed like what they must have wanted it to be, a refuge away from the world.

A few months later, for my birthday, Mom and Ray showed up at our house in Tucson with a new tailgate for my truck to replace the one I'd dented backing into the telephone pole. They'd found it at a wrecker. It was the most redneck present I could have gotten, and normally I would have cringed, but after that night out at the property I understood what it meant: even now that I was grown, she could still make things right.

In the clearing by my mother's trailer, we formed a circle by instinct, as if preparing to ward off an attack. I met my brother's eyes and we went to the door. The hinges creaked as a gust of wind blew it open a crack. Josh went first, opening the door and ducking through the entrance. I filled my lungs with fresh air and followed him.

Inside it was dim and warm. The smell wasn't as bad as I'd expected, musty and rich and a little sour, like the desert after a rain. A miniature kitchen ran along the far wall and sunlight slanted in from a small window above the sink. The cupboards and drawers had been emptied, their contents scattered across the countertops and floor. The cops had left a receipt for the evidence they'd taken: documents, pictures, a computer, a rifle, shell casings.

To my left a narrow hall led to the bathroom. To my right was the bed. I thought I'd get it over with and followed the buzzing of the flies. The mattress was gone, removed by the police. Past the headboard, a shelf stretched beneath the sloping roof of the trailer to form an alcove. The flies had gathered on the shelf. As I walked closer, I saw a milk crate full of papers, a few books, a small stereo I'd bought them for Christmas, and a large shadow that spread across the wood. The dark patch was larger than it looked from across the room, a rough circle a few feet in diameter. There was nothing else it could have been, but I didn't believe that it was blood, because there was too much. I touched the surface of the stain and my fingers came back caked with a brownish paste. I rubbed my fingertips together; it turned to powder and stained my skin. Where the pool was darkest, I noticed clumps of brown hair, and fragments of something I didn't want to identify.

A fly alighted on a photo album at the edge of the pool. I reached without thinking and picked it up. The caked blood around it crackled and flaked, and a piece of hair clung to the pewter cover until I brushed it away. It was my mother and Ray's wedding album. Blood had spattered across the bottom edge. I put it back on the shelf. Nearby lay a toppled bottle of holy water, also stained with blood. I put it in my pocket. I still have it in a box somewhere, and I still don't know why.

I got to work collecting what I wanted to take from that place. Josh was already sifting through the debris in the kitchen. I let my eyes roam around the trailer but had trouble focusing, couldn't find any one thing. I didn't want her clothes, her jewelry, her Catholic artifacts—what would I do with them? I didn't want any of the books because they were probably Ray's. I took the family Bible, a few trinkets I'd made or given her long ago, and all of the photo albums except the one stained with her blood.

Outside, I put the things in my truck and walked aimlessly downhill toward the gate, toward the road, toward nothing in particular. The only sounds I heard were the scuffing of my sandals in the dust, the pounding of my heart, and the sound of the desert, which I'd almost forgotten in the time I'd been gone: a murmur you can only hear far away from power lines and passing cars, like an unseen mouth breathing words into your ear. A length of yellow tape hung in a bush, printed with black letters: Sheriff's Line Do Not Cross. I took it, folded it neatly, and put it in my pocket with the holy water.

Miles down the valley, cars slid south on the highway, a string of distant strangers driving toward Douglas. None of them knew what had happened here. Neither did I. I knew the aftermath, some of the facts, what the police had seen fit to tell us. We'd know more once Ray was found.

I walked back up the hill to the clearing. Josh came out of the trailer. He gestured toward the barn. "Look around in there and take whatever you want," he said. "We're not coming back." We'd agreed to come here just this once, and to sell it as soon as we could.

I met Joe in the clearing and together we wandered the property, from the horse trailer to the barn to the storage shed, and gathered a haul. I took whatever I thought I might want to have, or whatever Joe suggested: a power drill, a set of tiki torches, an ice chest, and a gas-powered chain saw. I had no real use for power tools, and the backyard of our house in Tucson was choked with waist-high weeds, a bad place for flaming torches. I didn't need a cooler. I'd never used a chain saw in my life. But I took them anyway. In a few weeks we'd sell my mother's land, forty acres of empty desert, a shed full of ugly furniture and a barn full of moldy hay and a travel trailer where someone had been murdered, as a package deal at a bargain price.

While Joe was loading our new belongings into the truck, I stood in the clearing and took a final look around. It was a habit from my childhood: every time we moved, after Mom got divorced or flipped a house for profit, I'd take one last walk through the empty rooms. I told her I was making sure we didn't leave anything behind, but really I wanted to commit those places to memory, to remember where different versions of our family had lived and grown and split apart. I couldn't go back in the trailer, but as I turned away, I saw something in its aluminum skin. I walked closer. The metal bulged outward around a ragged hole the size of my pinkie finger. I stared at it for a long time before realizing a bullet had made it. A warning shot. Or a miss. Or maybe it had gone right through her.

My brother and grandfather had already begun to walk back to their car. On my way to the truck I saw Joe standing by a fire extinguisher that hung on the side of the barn. Hay stored improperly can combust, and the extinguisher was there just in case. I'd tried to tell Mom that if two tons of hay caught fire, an extinguisher wouldn't help; she might as well spit on the flames. But she kept it there anyway. Seeing it made me wonder if she'd raised her hands to stop the bullets.

Joe pointed at the fire extinguisher. "Might as well spray this."

"That's a good idea," I said. If the hay caught fire now, let it burn. There was nothing left to save.

He handed me the extinguisher. I pulled the pin and tossed it into the brush. One last time I looked: the blue mountains in the distance, the brown valley spread beneath them, the crumbling buildings of Gleeson up the road, the trailer, the clearing full of footprints, the tinkling wind chime she'd hung from the rafters of the barn. Josh was right; we'd never come back here. I squeezed the handle and sprayed, circling the clearing until the extinguisher was empty. As I turned to leave, the powder had already begun to settle, covering our tracks.

SCRABBLE AT GABALDON

————

After I moved away to college, my mother and Ray quit their jobs and sold the trailer where she and I had been living when they met. They said they were sick of working and wanted to travel. It wasn't a surprise; she'd been in that trailer for two years, and that was longer than she liked to spend in one place. In the thirteen years we lived in Tombstone, we called a dozen places home: houses in town, trailers on the outskirts, a couple of apartments, and, of course, the houses and trailers and apartments of her boyfriends and husbands. It got to the point where I stopped hanging posters in my bedrooms and kept my things in boxes, ready to load up and move whenever she decided to sell or break up.

Mom flipped a lot of property. She'd buy places and put them on the market again before we'd finished moving in, priced at ten percent higher than what she'd paid. She owned and ran five different businesses in Tombstone at one point or another. Her best friends were all real estate agents; she'd first met Bob and Connie when she bought a house from them. But it wasn't just houses: she refused to settle on any place or anyone. When I was a kid, the constant moving and changing bothered me. I told myself that when I was on my own, I'd find a home and stick, put down roots. But in the decade since I left Tombstone, I've had a dozen different addresses.

I hadn't expected her to stay in the same place after I left. But when she and Ray both quit their jobs, sold the trailer, and hit the road, I asked the obvious questions. How long would they be gone? What would they do for money? Where would they live when they got back? She waved my questions off, said I was too square. They were leaving the normal world behind. They called it the Adventure, a name my brother and I mocked. We got battered postcards and staticky calls from the remote reaches of America. Every few months they'd swing back through Arizona to visit for special occasions, Josh's graduation or my birthday. Their roaring, stinking diesel truck would show up in our driveway and they'd invade our house, set the dog loose in the backyard, take over our living room. For a weekend they'd complain about their self-imposed privation on the road and rave about how nice it was to have air-conditioning and running water. We'd eat a big dinner at a chain restaurant. Then they'd be off again.

After months of this, Mom convinced Josh and me to come visit them. They were camping for a few weeks along the Mogollon Rim in eastern Arizona, and she called and begged us to drive up until we both relented. We packed warm clothes and loaded my truck and set off on the four-hour trip to someplace called Gabaldon with only Mom's directions to guide us. On the drive, as we navigated the switchbacked mountain roads, Josh and I talked about how our mother had gone crazy.

"I don't know how long they think they can keep doing this," Josh said. We were crossing a bridge at the bottom of a steep canyon somewhere in the Pinal Mountains, near Globe. Far above us, the sun set over the rimrock. Down where we were, it was already dark.

"Forever," I said. "That's what they think. It's insane." We'd been at it for an hour, working each other into greater states of righteousness.

"We should talk to them about it," Josh said.

We tried to follow Mom's directions but they were typically unclear, relying on vague landmarks instead of road names and numbers—*turn right at the second fork after the tree that got struck by lightning*—and we arrived late to a remote expanse of land just off an Apache reservation, in a part of the state known for high school football, wildfires, alien abductions, and an apocryphal creature called the Monster. The sign for Gabaldon pointed into a stand of pines overlooked by the bare peak of Mount Baldy glowing in the moonlight. We drove in. The first four campsites were eerily deserted in the headlights, scattered with ash and half-burnt firewood. Just as Josh and I had begun to exchange worried looks, we saw the white horse trailer through the trees, and a flicker of firelight beyond.

My mother walked haltingly into the beams of light, shielding her eyes with a sideways hand, sticking to the side of the road, as if she were afraid of something. Maybe they'd gone feral way out here, away from civilization, started to view other humans as a threat. But she knew we were coming, and she had Ray with her: what was she scared of?

I parked my truck next to hers and Josh and I got out, hugged our mother, shook hands with Ray. Chance came padding over to lick my palm. We ate grilled steaks and baked potatoes wrapped in foil. After dinner we sat around the picnic table and played games in the harsh light of an electric lantern. Josh and I were on one side of the table, Ray and Mom on the other. Ray and Josh were drinking wine from a box. Mom and

I had water; she rarely drank and I pretended for her benefit not to be the binge-drinking college freshman I was. It wasn't late but the black ring of forest around us and the starry sky above made it seem like the middle of the night, and a vast silence gaped beyond the popping of the fire. It was easy to believe that there were no other people in the world but us, and I wondered if that was how my mother and Ray felt on their Adventure, spending so much time in places like these. I didn't think I could live that way, but I could almost understand why they did.

Mom suggested Scrabble. For an unschooled family—Josh and I were the first to attend college—we were pretty good at Scrabble. Mom didn't read much except for self-help and spiritual books, but she did crossword puzzles, had a thing for words. She had read to my brother and me in the womb, and she bought us lots of books, so we grew up reading: Josh was into war history, and I liked mysteries, adventures, Westerns.

Ray was not an educated man. He'd gone straight from high school to the Marine Corps. I sometimes saw him reading paperback versions of the classics—years later I would take a copy of Plato's *The Republic* off my shelf while I was moving, see his name inscribed on the inside cover, and throw it across the room—and I admired his impulse to self-educate, his curiosity about worlds beyond his own. I'd first been drawn to books by a similar desire to discover something beyond the bizarre hermetic world of Tombstone.

But Plato hadn't helped Ray's Scrabble game. He stared at the board for minutes at a time, lips moving, fingering his tiles, clearly overmatched. We should have taken pity on him. He could do things none of us could; he was a genius at the steering wheel, could back a horse trailer through a gate blindfolded. He just wasn't good with words. But Josh and I were long-warring rivals averse to mercy, and my mother had a nasty streak in competitions of any kind. And even though we all liked Ray, he was the latest in a long line of men, and the three of us treated him the same as we'd treated all the rest: he wasn't one of us.

We killed him. Somebody dropped a *Z* on a triple letter score. Mom had learned Arabic in the army, and she used one of those bullshit loanwords with a *Q* and no *U*. As the game went on, my brother and I started giving each other looks and smirking, and soon Mom joined in. By the end, the three of us were chuckling and Ray had gone silent. Mom beat Josh on the final turn. I finished third. Ray was a hundred points behind me.

When the game was over, Mom went to check on the horses. Josh walked off holding his cell phone above his head to find a signal. Ray lit his pipe and refilled his cup of wine. I hadn't been keeping track, but it wasn't his first refill. He sat across the table and stared at me. When he spoke, I smelled the acrid tobacco on his breath.

"I guess Scrabble's not my game."

I shrugged. "I lost, too." I felt bad for humiliating him. I rehashed all the things I'd told myself when I left her with him and moved away. He wasn't the enemy. He was a good man, or good enough: a marine, a cop, a protector. He treated her well from what I'd seen. So what if he wasn't good at Scrabble, if he got drunk once in a while?

"Maybe I should have gone to college," he said. I was looking toward the corrals, where shadow horses snorted and stomped, spooked by something they sensed in the night, and it took me a moment to realize that Ray was mocking me. I turned to him. His eyes were the color of shit. I'd seen this sour mood before, in other men, across other dinner tables. It was one of the first signs.

I thought of my mother out there in the dark, and wondered if she was watching us, if she was listening. She and I both knew that once the first battle began, there was no retreat. Apologies and retractions and promises were useless: in the end she'd have to choose between her man and her sons. In the past she'd always chosen us, but this time I wasn't sure she would.

I pretended that I hadn't heard him and changed the subject. I asked what he was reading. I don't remember what he said— maybe Melville—but it worked. We started talking books and we relaxed. The danger dissipated. Soon, over his shoulder, I saw my mother emerge from the darkness into the light of the fire. Another moment I come back to: I can still see her there, returning, her eyes rising to meet mine, the tiny smile, the shadows flickering across her face as she approached, reaching out a hand. I was so relieved to see her, as if she had been gone a long time. Her hand settled on Ray's shoulder and squeezed. He looked at me, and in the dim light I thought I saw a smile play across his mouth. Maybe he thought that he had won.

Josh and I never had our talk with Mom. From Gabaldon she and Ray left again, back onto the road, and we went home. We didn't see Mom and Ray again for months, but the postcards they sent told us where they'd been: Springerville, Arizona; Corona, New Mexico; Corpus Christi, Texas; Memphis; Oklahoma City; Paducah, Kentucky, which the postcard says is "halfway between Possum Trot and Monkey's Eyebrow"; Rapid City, South Dakota.

Sometime in those next few months she sent me a letter postmarked from Saint Louis and return addressed to a national park in Missouri. Four sheets of paper from a yellow legal pad, both sides covered in her looping scrawl, and except for brief notes on postcards, they're just about the only words she ever wrote to me. Before she met Ray, we never stayed apart long enough to need the mail.

She describes where she's writing from, their campsite in the Mark Twain National Forest near Bourbon, Missouri. She's sitting by a fire, writing in the light from a Coleman lantern and listening to country music on the radio. She says she's happy. *We have hay for the horses food for us & our dogs and a pen and paper to write to my darling—the basics in life and honestly—Justin— I couldn't be happier.* But after recounting their recent horseback adventures and telling me that their next stop is Kankakee, Illinois, she changes tack midparagraph, and suddenly she doesn't seem so content. She claims that the reason she's living primitively, without electricity or running water, is so that I can have tuition; she says she's sacrificing.

> The moral of the story is—you do not owe me— the choice is mine to make, just please take advantage of it. Understand, I would be much more comfortable taking a hot shower than a lukewarm 4 gal water bottle. . . . Not much my son.

And part of that is true: she helped me pay for school, and if she hadn't, it would have been hard for me to afford. The army sent her a check every month for a partial disability—she'd broken her wrist on a parachute jump gone awry—and she gave that money to me. Between that, financial aid, and the money I made working at the campus newspaper, I scraped by. But it's also true that nobody asked her and Ray to quit their jobs and traipse around the country aimlessly in what amounted to an early and reckless retirement. If they had chosen to live more normal lives instead, like the people they claimed to pity—with a steady job and a home address—then they would have had all those luxuries, like electricity and running water. She'd helped my brother pay for college, too, and she'd gotten by just fine. No matter what she chose to believe, she wasn't homeless because of me.

It's also true that my mother spent most of her life sacrificing for us: the C-sections, the long hours at work, staying in Tombstone so we could finish high school there, the money for college. My whole life, I watched her dreams die or be postponed—she wanted a third child, she wanted to see Europe—and I promised myself that one day I'd take care of her.

But she also loved to play the martyr. Whenever I got in trouble at school, I'd hear it: *I gave my whole life for you, and this is how you repay me?* In one breath she would say we didn't owe her anything, and in the next she'd list everything she'd suffered so that we could have a better life. Most of the marks on her ledger were true, but she also tried to pin her failed relationships on us; once or twice she even tried to claim that we were the reason she stayed through the abuse, as if we were the ones who wanted whatever sort of family we had with those men. There had to be someone to blame, and it was never her.

By the time she wrote that letter, she didn't have to sacrifice anymore. Josh and I were adults, living on our own. She could have finally lived for herself, done all those things she'd always talked about at the dinner table while she picked at her food and stared out the window: joining the Peace Corps, moving closer to the ocean. She was barely forty and she had some money saved and she was free; she could have done whatever she wanted. But she'd been sacrificing for so long that she didn't know how to live for herself, and so she gave up everything for yet another man. I couldn't understand then how she must have felt: alone and abandoned, as if nobody needed her. And there was Ray, a man adrift, a project. She played the martyr until she became one.

A REPRIEVE

A few hours after we left the crime scene, my dad flew into Tucsón, and I picked him up at the curb outside baggage claim, where he stood smoking a cigarette and talking to a stranger, gesturing at the saguaros planted there for tourists. Dad liked to make small talk; it was the only kind he was good at. I pulled over and honked but he just stared—he didn't know what vehicle I drove—so I got out of the truck and gave him a hug and loaded his bag in the back. I hadn't seen him in about a year but he looked the same as I remembered, nothing like me: a jutting chin, blue eyes a bit too close together. He blinks a lot, always looks like somebody's just taken his picture with a flash. He'd just turned forty-four, and I'd forgotten to send him a card.

We drove the streets of South Tucson in silence. When a family friend from Tombstone called my cell phone, I was so grateful for the distraction that I answered and listened for the umpteenth time in the last few days to condolences. It was a friend's father, a man I hadn't seen or talked to in years, and listening to his desperately sincere offers of help only made me angrier at my real father sitting across the cab from me, who had asked if I wanted him to come rather than just showing up, and then arrived too late to do much good. I knew I shouldn't blame him—at least he was making an effort—but I blamed him anyway. It was one thing my father was always good for: whenever something went wrong in my life, I could blame it on him.

We stopped at our house on the way to the hotel so Dad could see Josh. Some of our friends were over, so we all went out on the back porch and sat around cracking jokes and telling stories and avoiding the subject of my mother. Surrounded by friends and my brother and my dad, all of us sitting on mismatched lawn furniture and rusty weight benches and coolers turned upside down, drinking and bullshitting on the back porch late into the night, I was surprised by how easily I forgot what I'd seen earlier that day. The next day was Sunday, so there was nothing to do but rest, and that night felt almost like a holiday, almost like a party.

Hours passed. Somebody took Dad to his hotel, and our friends came and went. Soon there was only one beer left, and it was too late to buy more.

"If anybody takes that beer," my brother said, "there's going to be another murder."

Josh put his hand to his face after he said it and looked down at his feet. The circle went quiet and our friends exchanged glances. I found myself laughing out of sheer relief: if we could find a way to joke about Mom's death, maybe we would survive it.

Soon it was just Joe and me at a table full of bottles, passing a quart of tequila and smoking cigarettes. When the sky began to fill with light, Joe stood up and said he was going to bed. I told him I might stay out awhile longer; I was as tired as I'd ever been, but I didn't want to go to sleep because I was afraid of nightmares. I didn't want to see the inside of that trailer again.

Joe took a step toward the sliding glass door that led to the house, then paused and turned to me. His eyes were glassy from the liquor and bloodshot from lack of sleep. He'd been with us through everything. I knew he didn't want to leave me alone out there. He said that if I needed him, he was right down the hall. He looked up at the sky and shook his head. "It was a hell of a day. You should try to get some sleep."

I agreed. We walked inside, and he gave me a hug and went into his room. I went to mine and wound up where I'd been every night since she died: at my computer, too tired to focus, trying to think of what to write about what I'd seen that day, where to begin. I'd slept two hours in the past two days. My thoughts were so cloudy that I believed the worst was over:

I've done the hardest thing I'll ever have to do.

The next day Josh and I were sitting on our front porch watching cars drive by when our father walked up the driveway wearing sneakers, denim shorts, and a polo shirt with the logo of the company he worked for. He stopped on the step and stood in the shade with his hands on his hips. We were supposed to meet him and our grandfather at the hotel where they were staying in an hour.

"Did you just walk here?" Josh asked.

Dad nodded.

"That's like four miles," I said.

"I felt like taking a walk."

"It's a hundred degrees."

"It's not so bad," he said. His face was pink and sweaty as he smiled. "It's a dry heat."

Dad sat on the edge of the porch with his feet dangling in the row of dead plants our landlord had asked us to water. I thought about offering him my chair but didn't. A car passed in the street, the glare off its windshield blinding.

"Do you think you're safe here?" Dad asked.

It seemed like a stupid question: if any of us could have predicted what Ray would do, my mother would have been alive. Besides, we weren't going anywhere, and we all knew it. Ray would come and find us or he wouldn't. There was no point in talking.

"We don't even know if it was Ray," I said.

Josh drummed his fingers on the windowsill. "Who else would it be?"

"It could have been anybody," I said, although I knew he was right.

"You knew him best," Dad said.

Did I? I thought I had.

"It was him," Josh said. "It had to be him."

I didn't reply. It had been almost four days. Ray was still missing, and so was the truck. A helicopter search of the area hadn't found any sign.

Dad slapped his thighs. He was working up some wisdom. "I guess you never know what somebody's capable of."

The blinds in Grandpop's hotel room were drawn, letting in just enough light for us to see one another slouching on the twin beds, making desultory gestures. We were supposed to be discussing our plans for the next day, but nobody wanted to take the lead, and suggestions for action went ignored, silenced by the drone of the air conditioner. Josh and I were sick of talking. Dad didn't know what to say. And Grandpop was under so much stress that he kept confusing my mother's death with his second wife's less than a year before; he'd say his wife's name when he meant his daughter, conflating them into one long process of grief. The room wasn't helping—dim and cool and sealed off from the bright hot world outside, it felt as if we were sitting in a coffin—but none of us wanted to move. I didn't see how we were going to complete all these tasks when none of us could get up to turn on a light.

Despite all the things we could have worried about—the murderer at large, our own fragile states of exhaustion and stress, the unfathomable future—the most immediate problem was money. My mother's life insurance company was refusing to pay because her murder was unsolved, and we needed a lawyer, but we couldn't pay a lawyer without the life insurance money. We also couldn't pay for her cremation or funeral. Josh was a bartender and I worked part-time at the college newspaper for minimum wage; my primary source of income was Mom's monthly VA disability check, which would expire now that she was dead. Without that money, I couldn't make rent or pay my tuition. Grandpop lived on a fixed income. And even though Dad had already promised to send us a check when he got back to New Hampshire, we knew better. Dad's checks were always in the mail.

Our mother's will only made it worse. She had written it before she blew all her money on the Adventure: it was long and profligate, doling out more than a hundred thousand dollars among Josh and me, her mother, her brother Tom, and his kids. But as we were slowly learning with each phone call, whatever money she'd once had was gone: her bank accounts were nearly empty, she was carrying mountains of debt on her credit cards, and the only possessions she had to her name were a missing pickup truck and the land where she died.

Somebody suggested splitting up into teams: Grandpop with Josh, my dad with me. We could divide the duties.

I said I didn't like the idea.

"Fine," Josh said. "We'll take care of it. You don't have to do anything yourself."

He was probably being merciful, but that's not how I took it. "Fuck you."

"Take it easy," Dad said.

"No. That's bullshit." I jabbed my finger toward Josh. "I'm all you have left. Remember that."

"Stop being so melodramatic." He looked away.

He was right. I should have stayed calm, but I'd been losing patience. My brother and I had fought constantly as kids, and only when he left for college did we finally reach a détente. When I followed him to Tucson and moved into his house— he offered reluctantly, at Mom's insistence—we got along better, hung out together and treated each other as equals, and save for the occasional drunken arm-wrestling match or heated *Jeopardy!* argument, became friends. But now, when we needed each other most, I was regressing. I'd been picking fights with Josh, couldn't even talk to my dad, and could hardly stand to look at the abject sadness on my grandfather's face. My mother had held us all together. Now she was gone.

"I'll tell you what," Grandpop said. He took off his glasses, and as he wiped the lenses, he stared right through me. The skin under his eyes was dark and his face seemed made of paper. "There is no hell." He pointed at the floor. "Hell is here."

QUESTIONING

———

We pulled into the parking lot of the Cochise County Sheriff's Investigations Unit in the early afternoon. We'd already met with the lawyer, who'd told us that the life insurance wouldn't pay until the murder case was solved. We'd gone to the bank, where we withdrew what was left in her accounts. Later, we had an appointment at the funeral home.

The Investigations Unit was housed in a huge county services compound that had just been built on the east edge of Sierra Vista, in a patch of bulldozed desert bordered by trailer parks. The asphalt was black and spongy beneath our feet, the painted lines between parking spaces blindingly white. We took a concrete path that wound through xeriscape to a metal door with a window made of bulletproof glass, where we rang a buzzer and were let in by a receptionist. She was stern until we said who we were, and then she smiled sympathetically and asked us to have a seat, said it would only be a minute. I won-

———

dered if her kindness was part of a standard survivor treatment, something she learned in training.

A tall, lean white guy in a black suit walked into the room and introduced himself as Detective Freeney. He looked the part: he had a mustache and an air of gravitas, although he wasn't wearing a gun. He invited us into his office, which had a window facing north and not enough chairs. He went to get another. We all sat, and he began to ask carefully worded questions.

He asked if my mother had any enemies and we said yes, business rivals and ex-boyfriends, but not the sort that would want to kill her. He asked about my mother's past relationships. He wanted a complete history, with names and addresses. That took awhile. We tried to remember all of her exes, and argued over who came after whom, but we couldn't help him with addresses; we didn't know or care where those men went after they left.

He asked about her relationship with Ray. Everybody turned to me, because I knew him best; Josh had never lived with Ray, and Dad and Grandpop had both met him once. I told the story of how they met, and said how happy they had seemed together, that I'd thought he was an all right guy. I was pretty sure everyone else in the room had thought the same— if they disliked him, nobody had said anything when Mom was alive—but memories have a way of changing relative to context. We were beginning to remember clues that showed Ray was controlling, or that he had a temper. He was already becoming the villain.

Freeney asked if we knew of any marital disagreements between them and we said no, nothing specific. Grandpop said he'd noticed a strange tone in Mom's voice the last time they spoke on the phone. Mom and I spent most of our last conversation talking about terrorists, and the only odd sound I heard was static. But I didn't argue, because I knew that constructing a cause and effect would help make sense of the event we couldn't even bring ourselves to name. *What happened. That day. The thing.* Sometimes simply *it*. If we could convince ourselves that we might have seen it coming, might have prevented it from happening if only we'd been more aware, then we could still believe in an orderly and rational world. We wouldn't have to confront the likely truth: that a man we liked and trusted had shot my mother dead, and there was nothing we could have done.

As Freeney updated us on the status of the investigation, he mentioned an autopsy, and I realized that I didn't know how many times she'd been shot. I asked him.

There was a pause while he shuffled the papers on the desk in front of him. "Seven times."

We sighed and shook our heads in unison. Freeney asked his last question: he said they'd found a barrel full of empty liquor bottles at the scene. He wanted to know if Mom and Ray drank. I told him that our mother hardly drank at all. He asked if Ray was a drinker and I said not really, nothing heavy. As I said it, I thought of that Scrabble game and wondered if it was true.

What did I really know about their day-to-day life out there, remote and isolated, cut off from the telephone and the mail, with no TV and no Internet, just a radio full of Spanish? The quiet, the heat, the days that passed without seeing or speaking to another person. Living like that could have driven them to drink; I didn't believe it, but who could say? There weren't any witnesses to tell us what had happened. Until they found Ray, all we had were evidence and guesses.

Freeney said he didn't have any more questions. He thanked us for coming and said he was sorry for our loss, then shook our hands and gave us business cards. Before we left, he asked if we had any questions for him.

"What if Ray comes to our house?" Josh asked.

Freeney put his elbows on the desk and folded his hands in front of him. "I don't think it's likely." He paused. "But keep an eye out."

At the funeral home we chose an urn, picked out prayer cards, signed a series of papers, and answered the funeral director's question about whether her legal last name—Ray's last name—should appear in her obituary with a resounding no. During a brief silence, Grandpop thumbed a mint Life Saver from the pack he keeps in his shirt pocket and asked where she was.

The funeral director said she was in refrigeration. He didn't bat an eye when he said it; that guy was all business, and I liked him. He hadn't patronized or pitied us, and he called my mother by her name, not "the remains" or "the deceased" or any of that bullshit. He was an unassuming man, short and thickly built with light brown hair and glasses, unremarkably dressed. His job was not to be remembered, and he did it well.

Grandpop bit into his Life Saver. The lenses of his bifocals reflected the fluorescent lights above. "I want to see her."

Josh bowed his head. Dad just sat there.

"That's not a good idea," I said.

"I can bring the remains into the chapel," the director said evenly, "and you can have some time. But you should know that she was not embalmed, due to the autopsy."

I wondered where the chapel was. The funeral home was huge and labyrinthine; I'd almost gotten lost on the way to the bathroom. The director lived there with his family. His wife and kids were upstairs the whole time we were in his office, and we could hear their footfalls as they passed up and down the hall.

The director blinked and continued. "I have to warn you: there will be odor."

Somebody said Jesus. Somebody said fuck. Somebody repeated the word: *odor*. We convinced Grandpop not to do it. We finished the paperwork and Grandpop cut a check and Josh and I promised to pay him back, although we never would, and he knew it. Outside, in the cruel sunlight of the parking lot, Grandpop and Dad lit cigarettes. Past the mortuary sign and beyond the highway the Huachucas rose green to a cloudless sky, the mountain slopes a lush oasis where at that moment people were hiking and watching hummingbirds and smuggling drugs. As the others debated where we should get dinner, I stared at the funeral home's front door. I could still go back inside and ask to see her. It was the last chance I'd ever have; in a few hours she would be put in a cardboard container and burned. I wondered if I owed it to her, what she would have done in my situation.

And I wanted to know if I could take it. In a room inside that building the Beast was waiting; I wanted to face it to prove what kind of man I was. But I stood there thinking for too long, and we got in the car and left.

It was dark when Josh and I got home. We crossed our barren yard in silence and I held the screen door open, standing in the same spot where a few days ago he had told me she was dead, while my brother unlocked and opened the door.

Inside, our house was changed. The rug in the entryway had been shaken out. The floor tiles shone. The beer bottles and takeout containers had been cleared from the coffee table, and its surface was visible for the first time since I'd lived there. In the kitchen a week's worth of dishes sat drying in the rack, the counters bare and spotless. On the gleaming dinner table we found a note: two of our friends, Pete and Nolana, had cleaned our house while we were gone.

Such a simple thing, a small kindness; it almost brought me to tears. I turned on all the lights and stood in the middle of the house and thought of the Hemingway story I'd just read for my American lit class, the well-lighted café where waiters watch an old man drink alone late at night. The young waiter says the old man should kill himself. The older waiter tries to explain how it feels to be lonely, but nobody listens.

Josh called to thank Pete and Nolana and they came over. Joe came home from work and we sat in the living room. I walked into the kitchen to get another beer and when I came out, Josh made a crack about how I wasn't old enough to be drinking all the beer.

I knew Josh was only giving me a hard time, trying to act normally. But a senseless and indiscriminate rage had been rising inside me like a warm tide: rage at the professionals for their paperwork and their grim efficiency in helping us erase my mother; rage at the police for their failure to find the killer; rage at my family for our bumbling helplessness; rage at Ray for what he'd done; rage at my mother for her delusions—that harebrained life she tried to live, that ridiculous will—and most of all for dying. And rage at myself, for my own incompetence, for failing to prevent or remedy any of this, for being another angry, useless man.

I took it out on my brother, made a scene. I said things he already knew: that we were alone now, that she would have wanted us to be better to each other. My voice caught and I realized I was crying. Joe got up and came over to me, tried to calm me down, said Josh was just joking and everyone had had a hard day, to let it go. Everyone else turned their heads, avoided my eyes. Pity. So this was it: the sum effect of our mother's murder was that I should be embarrassed? Not sad, not overwhelmed by grief and fury—I was supposed to be embarrassed?

I went out to the porch, letting the door slam behind me, and sat on a plastic chair. The porch light cast a yellow ring halfway across the yard, but the street beyond was murky. I already regretted yelling at my brother. We were going through the same ordeal, but we couldn't talk to each other about it. In times of crisis, we'd always turned to my mother; whenever I needed help with schoolwork or had a job interview or broke up with a girlfriend, I'd go to her, and she'd talk me through it. The last few days what I'd wanted most was to be able to talk to her about her own death, to tell her the loss and emptiness I felt. She would have said what she always said, no matter how bad things got—she'd said it to me in hospitals, in courtrooms, in bedrooms down the hall from shouting men—even when I could tell she didn't mean it: *We'll be OK. We still have each other.* But she wasn't there to say it anymore, and it wasn't true. Now that she was gone, it felt as if a void had opened in the middle of my family, and we remaining men were standing on its edges, trying to shout across.

As I sat alone on the porch, I thought again of Hemingway— *nada y pues nada y pues nada*—and peered out into the dark street at every car that passed, gauging the shape of the headlights and the sound of the engine, expecting the bright rectangles and diesel roar of my mother's truck, for Ray to drive up our street and pull into our yard and run me over, crash into the living room, to kill us all and finish it.

FINAL GOODBYES

———

The morning of my mother's funeral mass, I pulled into the parking lot of the Sacred Heart Church in Tombstone a half hour early and sat staring at the basketball court behind the rectory where I'd played as a kid. The rim was low and bent by years of hanging boys. The steps of the church were empty. I'd stayed at a friend's house in Tombstone the night before, so I wouldn't have to get up early and drive down from Tucson. I was the first person there, and I wasn't sure what I was supposed to do, go stand under the plaster Jesus and hold the door open, sit in the front pew and try to weep. I wished I had a basketball.

I got out of my truck and smoothed the wrinkles from my shirt and walked to the entrance of the church. I went inside, blessed myself with holy water in the vestibule, and walked past the shuttered confessionals and a short way up the aisle toward the altar. My mother had tried to teach me the names of places in a church, the nave and crossing and so on. She had

———

gone to Catholic school and knew all the jargon, all the rituals; she used to sit next to me on Palm Sunday folding fronds into crosses, explaining the stations of the cross. She tried to raise me in the faith, but we only went to church on Christmas and Easter, or for a few Sundays in a row whenever she began to feel guilty. In the last years of her life she returned in earnest to Catholicism, started reading the Bible again, convinced Ray to convert, and cajoled me into taking classes to get confirmed.

I still have a picture from my confirmation, in a frame my mother bought and signed on the back in gold marker: *Congratulations Justin, xo Mom,* beneath a drawing of the Jesus fish. In the picture I'm kneeling at the feet of a priest who's about to rub chrism on my forehead in the shape of a cross and tell me to repeat his words accepting Christ and rejecting Satan. Ray stands behind me with his hand on my shoulder; he was my confirmation sponsor. My mother stands next to him, a bit behind. She's reaching for something, but the camera's angle hides her hand: it's not clear whether she's reaching for me or for him. That was the last time I'd been inside a church.

I went outside and stood on the sidewalk watching the sun rise, warming away the chill of morning. A green Dodge pickup parked across the street. I'd been gone for more than a year, but I could still identify most residents of Tombstone by their vehicles. The Dodge belonged to Dave, my mother's last boyfriend before Ray. He stepped down from the truck, straightened his bolo tie, and shrugged into his jacket. He was clean shaven and he'd tried unsuccessfully to tame his wild hair. I hadn't seen him since we'd moved out of his house. Now he was the first person at her funeral besides me.

Dave walked over. He asked how I was and I said all right, considering. We stood looking out at the cracked asphalt of Safford Street as cars parked and people in church clothes got out, pulling purses and coats from their trunks.

"I could never make her happy," Dave said abruptly. "I thought she'd found someone who could." The last words caught in his throat.

"I always liked you, Dave," I said. It probably wasn't much comfort, but it was the best I could do.

He put his hand up to shield his eyes from the sun. It looked almost as if he were saluting. The muscles worked along his jaw, and I knew he wanted to say more than that he was sorry, just like I wanted to say more than thanks, although that's all we said before he shook my hand and walked inside.

It was the first of many halting and deficient conversations I would have that day. Soon Josh and Dad and Grandpop showed up, and we stood for a while by the doorway, thanking the people who stopped to offer their condolences, until we realized we were only making things worse for everyone and went inside.

I was surprised to see the church half full. The funeral was held on a Thursday morning, and Mom didn't have much of a social life, so I hadn't expected a big turnout. I saw some friends from college and a few old friends from high school I hadn't talked to since I'd moved away. I saw the ex-girlfriend who'd broken my heart for the first time and wished she hadn't come. And I saw the families who'd helped raise us, our mother's few friends and our friends' parents, people who had fed us at their tables and cheered for us at baseball games and told us, over and over, to get the hell out of Tombstone the first chance we got. Half the people in that town had a hand in raising me, and it seemed like all of them were there.

But so were some of the other half, people who'd hardly known my mother, people she'd avoided because she'd been the victim of their gossip. You can't date as many men as she did in a town that small and hope to escape a reputation, the word the older boys on my junior high baseball team had called her to taunt me—*whore*—or the term a friend had overheard the town marshal call her while gossiping about her death in the Circle K: *black widow*. Now a lot of those same petty gossipmongers were at her funeral, wearing black, shaking their heads and dabbing their eyes and saying how sad it was.

The priest came out of the sacristy and I sat in the front pew next to my brother. I tried not to focus on the faces behind me aglow with pity. The brass box of my mother's ashes sat on a table in front of the altar. The priest was a hoary brimstone Jesuit my mother had disliked so much that she joined a different parish and drove all the way to Sierra Vista every Sunday rather than worship here. Whenever the Jesuit mentioned my mother, he looked at the urn, as if she were a jack-in-the-box waiting for someone to crank the handle. He flung some holy water and said it was time to say our final farewell to Deborah, and I bowed my head with the others.

The funeral director had offered us the chance to speak, and I'd tried to write something. But I couldn't do justice to her loss, so I'd declined. As I sat in that church with people I knew had been whispering her name, listening to a priest talk about judgment and redemption, I wished I had tried harder. I was lost in a fantasy of barring the doors and lighting the place on fire when a hand squeezed my shoulder.

I turned and saw a man's broad back disappearing down the aisle behind me. He was thick and tan and had a dark Mohawk. I couldn't see his face, but I knew who he was: my mother's only sibling, her younger brother. Uncle Tom.

When I was growing up, Uncle Tom would come stay with us for a while whenever he got fired or evicted, or whenever he'd blown all his money on drugs. Tom moved out to Arizona with his family a few years after we did, following his sister with the same idea: to start over. I was never told the details—I was too young—but I can guess why he moved. He had no job and a drug problem and a lot of old friends who didn't help in either respect, and North Philly was no place to be in the eighties, with the factories shut down and crack on every corner. If you had somewhere else to go, you went. Tom moved his family out West, thinking at least it would be different.

It was different; it was worse. Soon after they moved to Tucson, the first of his five children, Tom Jr., was killed by a car while crossing the street. His third child, a daughter, died in her crib during a nap. After that, Tom wanted to be closer to his sister, so he moved to Tombstone, a town with ten bars and no grocery store, smack in the middle of the biggest drug-trafficking corridor in America. It was the worst place in the world for an addict.

He spent the ensuing years in and out of our house, in and out of jail. My mother used Uncle Tom as a fuckup bogeyman through my years of teenage rebellion, when I was getting high every morning before school and drinking shoplifted tequila in parking lots at lunch. She'd come into my room at night and sit on the edge of my bed and say she knew what I was doing and wished I would stop, because she couldn't bear to see me turn out like Uncle Tom. I'd sometimes see my uncle at parties out in the desert, a figure on the far side of a fire, but we didn't acknowledge or talk to each other; I guess we were ashamed. He acquired the nickname Cool Breeze among Tombstone's slacker circles. Josh and I thought it was hilarious, but hearing it made Mom detonate.

The last time I'd seen Tom was after Ray moved in, a few months before I left home. I found my uncle sprawled across our yard-sale couch one day, wearing a sleeveless T-shirt, his Mohawk grown out into a black shock of tangled hair, still asleep at noon. I knew when I saw him that he'd be staying awhile—he always did—and I bitched and moaned a little about how long he spent in the bathroom, but otherwise I was OK with it. My first memory of my uncle is him telling me a dirty nursery rhyme, and since that moment I'd always liked him. But I made sure not to leave any cash lying around.

Ray didn't like Tom staying with us, and he didn't try to hide it. He rarely spoke to my uncle, and when Tom wasn't in the room, he'd start complaining. Tom didn't give a shit what Ray thought. He'd seen enough of my mother's men come and go, and he'd outlasted all of them, so he wasn't about to start kissing some cop's ass. Their grudge seemed too strong to be new; I wondered whether Ray had ever arrested Tom, although neither of them mentioned meeting before.

My uncle volunteered to help around the house, to earn his keep, as he put it. Which was how I wound up spending an entire weekend that summer with Tom, building a barbed-wire fence around our property. One of us would hold the fence post, trying to keep it straight, while the other beat it into the ground with a driver. It was a shitty job. The dirt of southeastern Arizona is hard and dry and full of cement-like rock deposits called caliche. Whoever held the posts had the driver tolling like a church bell right in his ear, and whoever swung the driver had to lift twenty pounds of steel a dozen times a post. It was a long fence that crossed uneven ground; it took a lot of posts. After a few hours we were both half deaf and hungry and sick of earning our keep.

At lunchtime, Tom and I sat on rocks and ate sandwiches. I told him about my new girlfriend, with whom I'd been antici-pating having reckless unprotected sex in my pickup truck that weekend until Mom had told me I had to build the fence. Tom listened to me gripe, but didn't say where he would rather be. We finished our lunch but didn't want to go back to work, so he started telling stories about his time in the army. I knew he'd been in the military but had never heard him talk about it. I was thinking of enlisting myself—my high school counselor had said it was that or community college—so I listened as he told me about a night he'd spent sitting in a guard shack somewhere in Germany. Snow was falling all around him and he couldn't see a thing, so he smoked cigarettes and drank whiskey from a flask until he fell asleep. He had a dream about enemies advancing through the snow. When he snapped awake, he thought he saw a person out there in the field.

Tom posed as if he were holding an invisible gun to his shoulder. "I'm fucking pointing my rifle and yelling at this dude, telling him I'm going to shoot, and then I look closer and there's nobody there." His bloodshot eyes flared wide. "I was about to kill nothing."

"Should I join the army?" I didn't typically ask my uncle for advice, but I thought that maybe if we dragged our feet enough, the sun would go down and we wouldn't be able to finish the fence, and Mom would either forget about it or make Ray do it.

"You can have a good time, man." He chuckled and looked off into the middle distance as if he were remembering another story. "I got to go all over the place, Germany and Europe. But there's always somebody telling you what to do."

That evening, after we'd finished working for the day, I walked down the hall of our trailer and found the bathroom door closed. I was about to knock when from inside I heard the squeak of a rubber band as it cinched tight, and then the telltale slapping. Soon there was a long sigh, and the toilet groaned as he slumped backward against the tank.

I sold him out. I didn't want my sketchy uncle shooting up in my house, so I told Mom what I'd heard. I came home from work a few days later and Tom was gone. I bet Ray did the talking when they kicked him out, and I bet he enjoyed it. For the rest of the time we lived there, I thought of my uncle every time I passed that slapdash fence, and wondered where he was, if he was all right.

The service ended. I tried to dodge the groping hands of the congregation to find Tom. He was hard to get hold of, with no steady phone number or address, and if I lost him then, I might not see him again for a long time. I thought I saw his Mohawk parting the crowd, and I called his name but he didn't stop. By the time I shrugged my way outside, he was nowhere in sight. I asked Grandpop and Josh if they'd seen him and they said no. I walked around the side of the church to the back, where a giant rosebush canopied the yard: I thought Tom might have gone there to be alone. But he'd vanished. I went back inside still feeling the weight of his hand on my shoulder.

In the aisle of the church, Tom's children—Leighanne and Sean and Eric, the three who had survived—were talking to my brother. I went over and hugged Leighanne, the oldest and my mother's favorite. The kids had lived with us on and off growing up, whenever the state took them away from Tom, and my mother often said Leighanne was like the third child she'd never had.

Leighanne kept glancing toward my mother's urn, still sitting on the altar beneath the empty pulpit. I hadn't seen her in a while, and I'd always thought of her as a little girl, but she'd suddenly become a teenager, willowy and pretty, red-haired and pale and preternaturally mature. Her face was calm and her eyes were steady; she understood. There would be no more weekends at Aunt Debbie's, no more horseback rides. Her brothers were younger, nine and eight, respectively, and they didn't seem to get it, kept fiddling with hymnals and casting restless looks around the room. I thought of their older brother, Tom Jr. I was about their age when he died; it was my first inkling of death. My mother answered the phone one day and listened for a few seconds before hanging up and bursting into tears. She sighed deeply, sat me down, and tried to explain in terms I could understand. If I could have remembered how she'd put it, I might have been able to explain her death to my cousins. I could have told them why they were standing in a church surrounded by adults, why their father had hurried away, why people kept looking at a brass box when they said my mother's name. But in order to do that, I would have had to grasp it all myself.

There was no burial afterward. We had decided to put her in the family plot in Philadelphia, and Grandpop was taking the ashes back with him to be buried later. After the mass, Bob and Connie invited us over to their house. As we pulled into their driveway, I eyed our old trailer next door, the spot by the carport where I'd said goodbye to her. I didn't recognize the cars parked there now. Somebody else lived there, strangers sleeping in our old rooms and eating in the kitchen where we'd shared the terrible pot roasts my mother cooked. It didn't seem right that it had been wiped clean like that, that we had been forgotten. I thought a place should have a memory.

Inside Bob and Connie's house I took a plate and filled it with food I wouldn't eat and sat on the couch. Everyone was talking about the murder, the troubles with the will and life insurance. Connie and Bob had known my mother better than anyone in the last years of her life. Connie was my mother's realtor and best friend, a gentle woman but one who got things done. Bob was a cowboy, a real one, not a poser like Ray: he'd worked on ranches as a young man, been a command sergeant major in the army, served in three different wars. He and my

mother had the kind of warm platonic relationship she sometimes had with men like him—strong, kind, respectful men,
men with nothing to prove—while she was running off and
marrying their opposites. Bob had found her body.

Somebody mentioned Mom's horses. Connie pointed out
the sliding glass door of their living room toward the corrals,
where a small herd of horses stood swishing their tails, but
instead I stared out into their backyard, where my mother had
married Ray.

Among the things we'd taken from the trailer where she died
was their homemade wedding guestbook: a few sheets of
computer paper folded in half and bound by two crooked sta-
ples. The cover has their names, the date and place—*Debbie &
Ray, May 13, 2001, Tombstone, AZ*—and a picture of the bride
and groom sitting in front of a blooming rosebush in Bob and
Connie's yard. The photo was taken with an early digital camera and printed on cheap paper, and the lighting is odd: sunlight bathes the rosebush and yard in the background, but
Mom and Ray sit in shadow in the foreground. The picture
looks almost fake, grainy and washed-out, the edges of their
bodies strangely sharp against the brightness beyond. Ray
wears a straw cowboy hat and his beard hides his unsmiling
mouth; he never smiled for pictures, was always playing the
tough guy. His eyes are slitted and inscrutable.

My mother wears earrings, thick gold hoops. That seems
out of character; she rarely wore earrings. I wonder if she
wore them because she was getting married, or if I remember
wrong, if I never knew her as well as I thought, if she was a
slate on which I wrote my own assumptions, as so many people are. The tiny line of gold below her neck is the crucifix she
always wore; that I do remember. I can't tell what her T-shirt

says: the first two words are visible, above a silhouette of horses and cowboys: *I'm a.* I'm a what? The smile on her face seems strained, but it's hard to say for sure.

The guestbook has ten pages. Seven are blank. The other three contain a half-dozen scrawled signatures I don't recognize, the laboriously printed names of my young cousins, and brief notes from Tom, my brother, and me. Tom wrote crookedly in letters of varying sizes: *Good Luck Always.* Josh added: *Congratulations & Best Wishes!!! Love Always.* I wrote: *Mom, it's wonderful to see you so happy. You deserve it.*

I don't remember much of the ceremony. I'd been to weddings involving both of my parents before, and they run together in my memory. I got dressed up, which, for a backyard wedding in Tombstone, the fifth wedding for the bride and the second for the groom, meant I wore a shirt with a collar. Josh wore a suit and tie even though he knew nobody else would, which was typical of him: Mom liked to tell stories of him as a boy, putting on a blazer to play in the street. My mother wore an off-white dress, and I think Ray wore a brown sport coat and jeans, although I have to rely on my memory, because the photos from that day were in the bloodstained album I left by the bed where she died. Leighanne was the lone bridesmaid. Josh and I were groomsmen.

As we stood waiting for the bride to walk up the aisle, I heard hoofbeats and turned to see a white pony trotting through a gate in the fence, pulling a small cart that carried my mother, with a young towheaded boy driving. The cart pulled up to the minister and stopped. I had never seen the pony or the boy before, although later I would learn that the boy was Connie's grandson. Josh and I did our best not to laugh as Mom stepped out of the cart and the pony trotted away.

She and Ray held hands throughout the brief service. Leighanne says my mother watched Ray the entire time, and that she shed a single tear and let it roll down her face without wiping it away. I don't remember any of that, but I do remember something the guestbook doesn't mention: they got married on Mother's Day. I'm sure Mom planned it that way. She must have thought having all of us there together on her special day would symbolize the new family she'd been seeking for two decades and through a handful of marriages. But even then it struck me as a strange day to get married. Now every Mother's Day I think of Ray's face on the guestbook, my inscription inside welcoming him into our family, and my words to my mother on her wedding day: *You deserve it.*

Before we left, Connie turned on the TV. She'd heard there would be something about my mother on the news. A Tucson station's intro played, shots of saguaros and the city skyline. We waited through a few stories about local events and the aftermath of September 11th, and then the name of my hometown appeared in the box in a cartoonish Western font. "And in Tombstone today," the anchorwoman said, "an Old West murder mystery." The camera panned down Allen Street, showing groups of pasty tourists and the sign for the O.K. Corral, as the anchorwoman discussed a murder that had happened fifteen miles from there. Her voice was high and hollow as she advised anyone with information to call the Cochise County sheriff. Connie turned off the television and we sat in silence.

"An Old West murder mystery?" I said.

We didn't discuss it again, but the next morning I looked up the network's newsroom number and called. Some poor intern answered. I yelled myself hoarse, throttling the handset, my voice quaking and tears welling in my eyes as I asked a stranger if he had any idea how it felt to have his mother's death on the evening news, described as an Old West murder mystery. When he found his voice, he apologized and promised to pass my complaint along to the producers. I never heard from them.

As we were leaving Bob and Connie's, they asked what we wanted to do with Chance. They offered to keep him, but even though he was Ray's dog, he'd become a part of the family. He was a good dog, obedient and protective, not a barker, never mean. And even if he would always remind me of his owner, that wasn't Chance's fault. I said I'd keep him.

I stopped at the Reischls' house on my way back to Tucson. Their oldest son, Marques, was my closest friend in Tombstone, and his family had always treated me like one of their own. Nobody was there—Marques was away at college, his brother was in school, and their parents had gone to work after the funeral. I went in through the side door, took my shoes off, and crossed the cool marble tiles to the guest bedroom, where I changed out of my funeral clothes and gathered the things I'd left there the night before. I went into the kitchen and thought about making myself something to eat—Julie cooked dinner every night, so their fridge was always full of leftovers—but I didn't have an appetite. Maybe I'd sit on the couch for a while and watch TV and wait for the Reischls to return. They'd told me their house was mine, but they didn't really need to tell me that, because their house had felt like home for a long time. In high school, when I left their place after staying for a few nights straight, afraid without reason that I might wear out my welcome, I'd turn into the dirt driveway that wound past Bob and Connie's house to our trailer and stop the truck and stare at the dim light shining in my mother's bedroom window, knowing she was probably waiting up, that she must have felt forgotten when she came back from work to that dark and empty trailer every night, and still I'd want to turn around and go back to the Reischls' and make up an excuse to stay another night.

I saw an envelope on the dinner table with my name on the front in Julie's handwriting. Inside was a sympathy card. She wrote that I was now part of their family, that they loved me like a son, and that she was there if I needed her. She told me to be strong. And she enclosed a check so that I wouldn't get behind on my bills. I hadn't told her that I couldn't pay the rent that was due in a few days now that my mother's VA checks had stopped coming—I hadn't told anyone, because I was ashamed—but somehow she had known.

I was sick of sympathy, the obligatory feel of the other cards and calls I'd received. But that small note in Julie's neat writing, reading it alone in their kitchen and feeling at home, it opened me right up. The last thing I remember from the day of my mother's funeral mass is sobbing in the house where I'd always wanted to live.

A BEAUTIFUL TIME IN MY LIFE

My dad flew home the morning after the funeral, and Grandpop left later that day with my mother's ashes in hand. We'd agreed to bury her in the family plot in Philadelphia sometime in December; until then, the urn would sit on Grandpop's dinner table. The sympathy cards stopped coming in the mail and our phone stopped ringing. Josh and I went back to work, and I tried to salvage what credits I could for the semester. We didn't hear from the police. The life insurance hadn't come in, so we were still broke. Our lives were eerily the same as they'd been before, except that our mother was dead, and the only suspect in her murder was still at large.

After everyone else had gone home, my uncle Norman knocked on our door one day, carrying a sixer of Michelob in a plastic bag. He'd flown to Tucson after my mother's funeral mass. He said he wanted to be there to provide emotional support for my brother and me. The timing of his visit didn't make a lot of sense to us, but we weren't exactly surprised. Nothing Norman did surprised us anymore.

Technically, Norman wasn't even our uncle. He was a second cousin on my father's side. But he got along so well with Mom that we'd always known him as Uncle Norman. He was a character: portly and exuberantly gay, frenetic and profane, with enormous Coke-bottle glasses and a thick New England accent. He smoked two packs of Kools a day, and once, when my mother had hooked him up to our home heart monitor, his pulse had registered at ninety beats a minute. His open homosexuality had made him an outcast from my father's family, and might have explained why he bonded with my mother, who had a soft spot for outcasts. When Norman came to visit, they'd stay up talking through the night.

I'd always liked Norman; when I was a kid, we'd go for long rides on his motorcycle and talk about my loser dad. Norman even moved from New Hampshire to Tombstone at one point—Mom convinced him, as she had with Uncle Tom—but it didn't take long for him to see that it wasn't a good place to be an outspoken gay man, and after a few months he moved to San Francisco.

I hadn't seen him much since then, so I appreciated the fact that he showed up, even if he was too late. I gestured toward the plastic chair next to me and took the beer he offered, although it was the early afternoon and I was still hurting from the night before. He sat, pulled a pack of Kools out of his pocket, lit one, and said he wanted to talk to me. I told him I didn't want to talk anymore. She'd been dead for days. There was nothing left to say.

Norman took a drag, blew a stream of smoke, and surveyed the wasted lawn. He said he'd spent the last couple of days driving his rental car through rural Cochise County, looking for Ray, which seemed odd considering that as far as I knew, they had never met. Norman had talked to every cop and by-stander who'd humor him, asking if they'd seen a man matching Ray's description driving a red Ford pickup. It seemed ludicrous and maybe dangerous for a man like Norman to travel the remote reaches of Arizona interviewing strangers, but it made me wonder if that wasn't what I ought to be doing instead of lying awake at night with a rifle by my bed, waiting for Ray to come to me.

Norman said one old man had seen a red Ford headed south toward Mexico. I told him there were shitloads of red Ford trucks in rural Arizona. He leaned forward until his tank top tented out from his chest and set his elbows on his knees.

"I went out there," he said.

"Out where?" He didn't reply. "You went to the property?"

"I didn't go inside." He drank from his beer. "But he was there."

"What?" Norman was staring off into the distance, and I wanted to wring his neck. Who was where? Dead or alive? And did he need to be so theatrical about it? "What do you mean he was *there*?"

"I felt his presence."

"Jesus Christ." I slumped against the chair. I'd had so many talks with so many people, my family and the mourners and funeral directors and cops and lawyers, asking the same questions and getting nowhere. The last thing I needed was a psychic.

Norman set his beer down on the concrete. "Don't you ever feel his presence?"

Of course I did. I felt Ray's presence like I felt my mother's absence, everywhere and all the time. Every truck that drove past in the street at night, every time I saw a balding head across a crowded room, every time I saw John Smoltz make another save on *SportsCenter*. Ray looked uncannily like

Smoltz, a pitcher for the Atlanta Braves, a team I already loathed for constantly beating my Phillies. I had never put my finger on the resemblance before my mother's death, but now the sight of Smoltz's face sent me into a rage.

"He's still around," Norman said. "I can tell."

A few days later, Norman left. When we said goodbye on the front porch, I didn't know that I'd see him only one more time, at a family reunion a year later, that we'd sit at a picnic table drinking late into the night, telling stories about my mother, how he still thought he heard her voice sometimes, and how I didn't. Or that he would call me months later asking for help with his rent, saying I was his last chance, and I'd give it to him and never mention it again, and neither would he, but after that things would never be the same between us. Or that years later I'd learn in a phone call from my father that Norman's poor overworked heart had given out in an apartment somewhere in Texas, that he had been discovered dead and alone, like too many of my family members.

About a week after my mother's death, I went back to Tombstone for a football game. Marques was home from college for the weekend, and we wanted to watch his little brother quarterback our alma mater in its homecoming game. It was a mistake. At the gate, my old PE teacher gaped at me as if I were a ghost before waving off my entry fee. Customers in line at the concession stand turned to watch me walk past. I kept my eyes ahead as we climbed the bleachers to where the Reischls sat at the very top. I knew I was being watched; the field lights were blinding, as if I were onstage, and my steps rang out on the metal stairs. A low murmur followed in my wake. I sat flanked by Marques's family for the entire game. At halftime we risked a trip to the cross-country team's bake sale. En route, an old neighbor collared me to say that she'd always known there was something wrong with Ray, that she'd never liked or trusted him, and then stood there waiting for me to congratulate her on her hindsight. Voices said my name as I passed, but I kept going. At the bake sale I saw a friendly face, a former teacher and coach. He gave me a brownie and I stood next to him. He asked about Tucson and school. Then he reached over and squeezed my shoulder.

"Tough week," he said.

"I've had better."

I stayed there in the shadow of a lightpost for most of the second half, watching spectators pass by sneaking looks at me. In my hometown I'd become a perverse kind of celebrity, the victim's son. For a long time after I'd moved away, I missed Tombstone, and often fantasized about returning. But that night I realized I could never go back.

A month passed. The life insurance didn't come. We sold Mom's horses and one section of the property, let the banks foreclose on the rest. I continued a binge of drinking and carousing and banal self-destructive behavior. I stopped writing every night; I had nothing interesting to record, and I'd lost my urge for preservation. Still no sign of Ray.

I woke one morning in late October and remembered that it was Josh's birthday. It would be our first family occasion without my mother. I lay in bed for a while, trying to fall back to sleep, and then got up and wrote my first journal entry in weeks. In it, I wondered what I should get Josh as a present, when all either of us wanted was Ray. I still imagined he'd be caught alive, and had fantasies of retribution: watching him die in the gas chamber, shooting him myself. I don't know why I assumed I'd be capable of killing someone. It may have been the effect of all that Tombstone lore: I thought I'd get my showdown, and in my righteousness I would prevail, like Wyatt Earp. So I kept the rifle ready and waited for Ray to appear.

For my brother's birthday we went out to dinner at an Italian restaurant with a group of friends, and afterward we went to the French Quarter, the same place we'd gone the night we heard the news. We drank pitchers of beer and did rounds of shots, fed dollars into the jukebox—my brother has an inexplicable fondness for Elton John—and arm-wrestled one another and told jokes and did our best to have a good time. The night ended with Josh climbing up onto the stage and dancing, a tall, sweaty man with his shirt untucked swinging from a pole to "Tiny Dancer." The rest of us laughed in relief: there he was, the Josh we knew. He was going to be all right.

Somebody took a picture of my brother and me that night. Josh and I sit next to each other at a table, with strings of bar lights glowing behind us, a neon beer logo reflecting in a window, and a souvenir Bourbon Street sign barely visible in the top left corner. We're both drunk and bathed in camera flash, our faces flush and narrow-eyed and grinning, drinks in our hands. We look like what we were trying to be at that moment, two brothers celebrating. Josh is turning twenty-four and I'm still too young to legally be in that bar. Our mother has been dead a month and we're smiling. We've learned how to pose.

Two months after my mother died, I went on a date. Her name was Eliza. We worked together at the newspaper. After building up the courage for a few flirtatious weeks, I asked her to go to a football game with me. By halftime, Arizona was losing by thirty and she'd confessed that she hated football, so we left to get dinner. We wound up at a concrete table in a strip-mall parking lot, eating frozen yogurt and talking about our families. She told me what her parents did. I said I didn't really have a dad and that my mother had passed away. I already hated that phrase, but it was better than the alternatives.

Eliza eyed me over her yogurt cup and said she was sorry. I said thanks.

"How long ago?" Her green eyes were wide, her face curious and concerned.

"A couple of months."

She twirled her spoon. We didn't say anything for a while.

"How'd she die?"

"My stepdad shot her."

The spoon stopped halfway to her mouth. Tears welled in her eyes. I handed her my napkin. It was the first time I'd had to tell anyone I was dating, and I'd handled it all wrong.

Later that night she and I took Chance for a walk. My neighborhood didn't have streetlights, so as we walked I saw her face only dimly, in the lights of neighbors' porches. At first we didn't say much. I thought I'd ruined the entire night by telling her, and told myself that next time I'd wait longer to have the talk. Next time I'd lie: car wreck, cancer.

As we walked in silence, the sounds of the neighborhood sharpened: cars racing down Speedway, sprinklers in the park stuttering, the gravel scattered at the mouths of driveways crackling beneath our shoes. I brought up work and school and plans for the future, trying to change the subject to typical first-date topics, but everything I said sounded sadder than it would have before I told her.

We stopped at a neighborhood park and I let Chance off the leash to run. Eliza and I sat on a swing set and watched the dog dart across the dark field. Chance caught a scent and tracked it to the street, but lost the trail at the curb and raised his nose to the wind, trying to find it again. He trotted back and forth, sniffing. Whatever he had smelled, he wanted it badly. I wondered if he was searching for his master, just like everybody else was.

Ray once told me the story of how he found Chance. He'd seen a dog walking alone on the shoulder of a highway, picked him up and taken him home. The dog didn't have any tags, didn't try to leave, and seemed friendly enough, so Ray decided to keep him. Ray played the hero, like he did in most of his stories: he figured he'd given the dog a second chance at life by saving him from being hit by a car or attacked by coyotes or starving to death in the desert. So that's what he named him. Ray was a literal man.

When he fled, Ray didn't take Chance with him, which was partly why I had trouble believing at first that he'd done it. Later, it made sense. Ray was in a hurry, and Chance would have slowed him down. Still, Chance must have tried to jump into the truck, like he always did. He must have whined and barked. How does a man who just murdered his wife treat his dog? Did he kneel down and pet Chance one last time as he said goodbye? One thing's for sure: Ray didn't shoot him. He left a witness. I wonder if that's why we decided to keep Chance, in some vain hope that one day he would speak.

At our house, Chance was not himself. He slept constantly, pawed at our bedroom doors at night because he hated to be alone. He hardly ate. In his sleep his legs would twitch as if he were running in a dream, and from the way he whined, I knew he wasn't chasing some imaginary rabbit—he was running away. Chance spent his waking hours curled in the doorway, watching the road. But even though I knew he was suffering, and it must have been hard for him to adjust to the new world he'd found himself in, I was also glad to have him: if Ray arrived, Chance would warn us.

During those months when Ray was missing, while my attention lapsed in a lecture, or while I was waiting for the final pages at work, I'd sometimes find myself daydreaming about what he might be doing at that moment. I'd picture him on a beach in Baja, drinking margaritas and dodging the *federales,* scanning the sand for his next victim. Or I'd imagine that he was holed up in the mountains outside of Tombstone, hunting deer in the rocky canyons of Cochise Stronghold, where the famed Apache chief had evaded capture for years. Or I'd see him parked at the end of our street, staking out our house, the embers in his pipe painting his face red.

But as time passed, I thought of him less and less. I tried to focus on other pursuits. I caught up in my classes, worked late nights at the paper, started going to the gym, cut down on my drinking. The insurance money finally came in and I was suddenly flush with cash I didn't want but couldn't afford to turn down, so I paid off my debt and bought the Jeep I'd always wanted and took Eliza out to dinners, movies, concerts, wherever we wanted to go.

I began to make friends with my coworkers at the paper. I'd started as a copy editor, proofing articles for grammar and AP style, but when the sports editor asked me to work for him, I leaped at the chance to write about something beyond my own grief. For the first time I was seeing my name in print, and I wrote less and less in my journal. When I did, the entries rarely mentioned Mom. One from December 8, 2001, narrates a party I'd attended with Eliza the night before, thrown by coworkers from the newspaper. The first line reads: *This is such a beautiful time in my life.* My mother wasn't buried yet, and her killer was still missing.

The very next day, December 9, a New Mexico state policeman called Detective Freeney and told him he'd found a man's decomposing body in a red Ford pickup, next to a suicide note and a driver's license for Duane Raymont Hudson. Freeney must have called Josh, and Josh must have told me, and I must have been relieved. But I don't know for sure how I heard, or how I reacted, because I can't remember anything about the moment I learned that Ray was dead, and I didn't write a word about it in my journal. I must have thought that I could finally forget.

THE FAMILY PLOT

A week before Christmas, I rode with Grandpop and my brother to the family plot in a cemetery on Cheltenham Avenue, just beyond the city limits of Philadelphia. It was cold and gray and damp outside, good funeral weather, and Grandpop narrated directions as he drove: *Left at Felix Hanlon; remember that, left at Felix Hanlon.* He said it was in case we wanted to go there on our own sometime, but we knew he was telling us so we'd know the way when he was dead. He didn't need to say it: I was expecting him to die, because since my mother died, I'd expected death to come to anyone at any moment and thought I should prepare.

Grandpop parked his Caddy on the shoulder of the ink-black graveyard lane, behind a white truck with shovels in the back and two men inside the cab who didn't turn to look when we arrived. We got out of the car and Grandpop opened the trunk and lifted out the urn. The family mausoleum was a few feet from the road, a stone vault with verdigris doors and a stranger's name engraved above them, some long-forgotten relative. Flat black gravestones ringed the granite walls, bearing the names of other relatives I never knew. A canvas tarp covered one of the graves near the back of the plot, next to a lawn-mower path.

Grandpop set the urn near the edge of the tarp, backed away, took a camera from his jacket pocket, and motioned at my brother and me to close in on either side. He wanted to take a picture of us with our mother's ashes. I turned to Josh and saw that his lips were pinched together, bloodless and white. We took our places and Grandpop backed away, trying to fit two tall men into the frame with a small urn lying on the ground. He took the picture. I never saw it.

Others began to arrive. Our grandmother was dressed smartly in all black, her blond hair perfectly coiffed, her elegant high-cheekboned face like chiseled marble. I saw a few strange faces but didn't introduce myself. It seemed odd to me that my mother had an entire life before the one we had together. These people remembered a different person, the person she had been before I was born, a child and a girl and a young woman I never knew and wouldn't recognize.

The priest was late. As we stood around glancing at our watches, I let my anger well and fester. A self-indulgent, blinding fury had become my default response to any official ineptitude, real or imagined. It didn't matter that I could see from where I stood how much traffic there was on the avenue, or that it didn't make a difference what time we buried her, or that I didn't believe the words he was going to recite over her ashes. The tardy priest was another sign of the injustice of the world.

I'd voted against the burial service. She'd already had a funeral mass in Tombstone, and in a few more days she would have been dead three months; it felt like forever. When I saw something that reminded me of her—a horse on television, a woman with similar hair across a restaurant, a mother on the sidewalk pushing a stroller—she would glimmer in my mind, and I'd will her away. I was building walls in my memory to separate the present from the past, walls to hide her, walls to keep the Beast away. I didn't want another ceremony or the false comfort it offered. But there we stood, surrounded by stone angels, waiting for a priest.

My grandmother had a bunch of plastic roses in one hand and a cluster of balloons held by their strings in the other. She handed one of each to everyone and told us to take turns walking to the grave, laying a flower on the tarp, and releasing the balloons into the sky. When it was my turn, she held out a flower.

"I don't want one."

She lifted her hand higher. "Take it."

I thought about refusing. My mother wasn't looking down at us, watching her own burial, and she didn't hear our goodbyes or feel our fingertips tracing the freshly etched letters of her name. She was gone, forever, and I wasn't going to waste any more time wallowing in grief. I didn't want prayers, flowers, tears; I just wanted it to end. But my grandmother looked tired—we all were—so I took the flower and set it down, took a balloon and let it float away into the sky.

The priest finally showed, sprinkled some holy water, said a prayer. I was looking out over the long green lawn of the cemetery, down the slope of the hill to where a mist hung over the faraway graves, when I realized it was over. The priest shook hands with Grandpop. The others walked past the grave a final time and headed for their cars. I went to her grave and looked down at the stone:

I had to read it twice to understand why it looked odd: she was buried with my father's last name. She'd gone by his name for most of my life, whenever she wasn't married to somebody else, and sometimes when she was. She always said she wanted the same name as her sons. Grandpop must have made the decision not to use her maiden name. He'd chosen our last name instead of his. Seeing it etched in stone felt vindicating, as if from the moment she'd become our mother, she'd belonged to us. Still, it didn't seem right that even in death she'd be marked with the name of a man—my father—who abandoned us, a man who wasn't even at her funeral.

I lingered at her grave, waiting for something that didn't come: no revelation, no Beast, no sense of closure. When we pulled away in the Caddy, her urn was still sitting on the tarp. The gravediggers leaned against their truck, waiting until we were gone to bury her.

Dead people belong to the live people
who claim them most obsessively.

—JAMES ELLROY

NEIGHBORS

A t the edge of the city the fog breaks and reveals that
strange San Francisco sunshine, soft and buttery,
hardly even warm. It's Sunday afternoon and I'm
driving south, weaving through light traffic on the freeway,
listening to NPR, drinking fair-trade coffee from a place called
Progressive Grounds. It might be one of those snapshot moments I often have since moving to California—is this my new
life?—if I weren't going to a graveyard. I recently read a biography of Wyatt Earp that said he was buried in Colma, a few
miles from where I live now, and thought I'd pay my respects.

When I lived in Tombstone, tourists disappointed at Wyatt's
absence from Boothill Graveyard would sometimes ask where
he was buried. I didn't know. I didn't give a shit back then; I
was sick of hearing the stories. Only long after I moved away
did I take an interest. Now I've read a shelf of books about
Wyatt and Tombstone and the Gunfight at the O.K. Corral,

----

and I've seen the movie *Tombstone* so many times I can quote it by heart. I'm practically an expert on Wyatt Earp.

He's buried in a Jewish cemetery, in his third wife's family plot, although he was the grandson of a Methodist preacher and not a religious man himself. I park at the cemetery entrance and wander the rows for half an hour before I see his stone, tall and black in a field of gray, facing West, bearing his full name: Wyatt Berry Stapp Earp. The original marker was small and flat, like the ones around it, but it was stolen in 1957; by then he'd become a legend, so somebody bought him a bigger tombstone. An empty shooter of whiskey, a bullet casing, and a miniature American flag lay atop his grave, a shrine to someone's idea of him. There's not much of a view: at the bottom of the hill blank stones wait outside a mason's shop, and across the street a SuperTarget sprawls along the freeway. I wonder if Wyatt ever thought he'd wind up here.

After the gunfight made him famous, he left Arizona to rove the West, chasing mining booms, gambling, barkeeping, racing horses, bounty-hunting. A decade later he settled in San Francisco, where he had a beautiful wife, a steady job that didn't get him shot at, important friends. He didn't talk much about his past in Tombstone, although it caught up with him eventually, as it always would. He later said those first few years in San Francisco were some of the happiest of his life.

I moved here two years ago from Arizona, and I've also found a better life: a career, a woman who loves me, smart and successful friends. I take public transportation, eat organic produce, have business cards and a coffee grinder and a roommate from France, hang out at used bookstores and lesbian bars and literary readings. I've come a long way from Tombstone, and I should be happy. But this life feels like a lie, because it's built on one. When I moved here, I denied my mother, lied about her death, kept her pictures in boxes, tried not to think of her. I thought I was leaving all that behind, starting over. It worked, for a while.

Then one night I found myself talking to a friend, Laura. I'd met her just after moving to California, and wanted her right away: big brown eyes and a Tennessee accent, from a factory town in Appalachia, a poet with a wiseass sense of humor who spoke fluent French. She wasn't single and her parents were still alive, but nobody's perfect.

We were standing on a fire escape outside a party, talking about relationships. I mentioned a girl I'd been seeing casually, said she was pretty and smart and fun, but her parents were both doctors and she was a slightly different kind of doctor, and she'd gone to Stanford and she drove a Benz, and I couldn't get past my grudge against people like that enough to date one. Laura said she was going to break up with her boyfriend.

Voices drifted out from the party. Beyond the railing of the fire escape, the gray rooftops of Bernal Heights rose crookedly up the hill. As the silence stretched, I felt my opportunity passing, but before I could bring myself to say how I felt about her, Laura asked about my mother. I'd told her long before that she'd died in a car accident. It wasn't the time to come clean, standing out there in the gusting wind.

"My stepdad shot her."

For a moment, Laura didn't say anything, just stared searchingly at my face. "That's awful," she said, and left it at that. We talked about something else and went inside. Soon afterward we started dating. It wasn't like I'd feared it would be; she didn't ask a lot of questions or define me by my past.

Afterward, I wondered why, after lying about my family to everyone I met in California, I had blurted my secret to a woman I liked at a party. It didn't make sense, but it wasn't a surprise; lately I'd felt the walls around the past crumbling, sensed something stalking me again. Standing on a dais at my brother's wedding, about to give a speech in which I wouldn't say her name, I caught myself looking for my mother's face in the crowd. After a day spent flying kites with a friend and her daughter, I stood in her kitchen watching them build a house together out of Popsicle sticks and remembered for a moment how it was to have that bond. On Mother's Day I lay in my bed, thinking of the gun I keep beneath it, wondering how it felt to die that way. For years now I've denied my mother's murder, always trying to be some different kind of man— normal, stable, calm. I've hoarded the rage in my heart, and it manifests in the destructive ways rage does: chronic chest pain, failed relationships, an exaggerated response to threats. I expect the people I care about to die at any moment, and I don't make plans for the future, because I don't believe in it; in order to do that, I'd have to understand the past. Running from it has only brought me here, to a graveyard at the end of the West, still watching for the Beast out in the weeds.

My mother is buried beneath another black stone on another hillside, a few thousand miles east. I don't visit her grave. She fades a little more each day: I can't picture her face, can't remember a time when she was alive. I don't know her story, because I've tried to forget, and because there was so much I never knew. She didn't like to think or talk about the past, a trait I inherited. Nearly a decade now since she died, and all that's left of her are a few relics and my own suspect memories. I know more about Wyatt Earp than I do about my mother.

She was born Deborah Ann Bennis in North Philly on August 10, 1957, to teenage parents from working-class Catholic stock. When my grandmother got pregnant at seventeen, my grandfather did the honorable thing: he married her and joined the military. They gave it a shot for a few years, living on air force bases—West Palm Beach, then Belleville, Illinois—but soon they moved back to Philly and divorced. Neither of them can explain why, and when they see each other now, which is rarely, they act like the lovebird teenagers they once were, although both insist they never should have gotten married. My mother lived with her mom, seeing her dad on the weekends. He would take her to a pond near his house to feed the ducks. He says she was so tiny, they were bigger than her.

My grandmother remarried, had my uncle Tom, and got divorced again. My mother lived with her mother and brother for the next decade, in different houses with different men. That period of time was never mentioned in later years; my grandmother still won't talk about it except in the vaguest terms. Once, at a family reunion, a distant aunt sat next to me, patted my knee, and said my mother had it rough growing up. "There are a lot of things you don't know," she said. But she wouldn't tell me what they were.

At thirteen my mother showed up at my grandfather's door in the pouring rain, soaked and frowning, holding a suitcase. She'd said she wanted to live with her father one too many times, and finally her mother had dropped her off. Grandpop was working full-time for a union, living with his siblings in a house they'd inherited when their parents died. There was nowhere to put a teenage girl, so he sent her to a Catholic school north of the city, where she lived with the nuns for a year. He says she hated it; she was the only boarder, woke up with the nuns, had breakfast with the nuns, was schooled by the nuns, nuns nuns nuns. She told Grandpop she didn't know why he was punishing her. He told her one day she'd have kids and she'd understand.

After a year of picking her up every weekend and bringing her home, hearing her complain about boarding school, Grandpop bought a condo and my mother moved in with him.

In public school she twirled a baton, chased boys, got into trouble. Grandpop says he came home once and found some burnout boyfriend sitting on his couch, drinking a beer; the boyfriend offered him one and Grandpop kicked him out. At fifteen my mother was picked up in Washington, D.C., by a cop who saw her walking down the street with her best friend at two in the morning. She'd been hitchhiking to Haight-Ashbury. That was 1973, Grandpop says, a little late for the free love, but she didn't know that. She didn't know much. He let her stew in the holding cell for a night and sent bus fare.

At seventeen, as soon as she could, my mother joined the army, the best way out of Northeast Philly for a working-class kid. She met my father in the service. The way he tells it, he'd just returned from a year in Korea, patrolling the DMZ in a tank, when in the mess hall at Fort Knox he saw this girl, real pretty, walking out the door by herself. He turned to the guy next to him and said he was going to go talk to her.

He once gave me a picture of them on their wedding day, standing at the altar. On the back is a handwritten date: February 5, 1977. My father wore a white tux with bell-bottoms and a bright red shirt with ruffles, a white bow tie, and white boots. My mother's white dress had sleeves of flowered lace and she wore a wide-brimmed hat that looks plastic. They were nineteen. I knew that as a fact, but never understood what it meant until I saw the picture, their faces smooth and scared. I was about that age when she died.

Eight months later my brother was born. My parents got discharged and moved to Philadelphia, next door to my great-grandparents, across the street from Olney High. My father once told me the address, and the last time I was in Philly, I went by it, a run-down row house in a rough part of town. I was probably conceived on the night the Phillies won the 1980 World Series. She read to me in the womb.

One night while she was pregnant with me, a man broke into our house and robbed it, stole the family silver. My father says he heard a noise in the night, saw a shadow, and sprang out of bed to protect my mother and my brother. He yelled and the man in the dark retreated into the alley. My father tried to chase him, but he was already gone. My mother told her version of the story once, long ago, and I don't remember the details—a knife, a greater sense of danger—but my father wasn't the hero.

I was born, a C-section, my mother's second; she hemorrhaged, had an emergency hysterectomy, and her dream of a third son died on the operating table. We moved to the suburbs. My parents' relationship, already strained, began to crack; my grandmother says my father was a feckless drunk, unemployed, getting high. One day my mother found my four-year-old brother walking shirtless down the middle of the street, my father passed out on the couch. She reenlisted. We moved to North Carolina. It was a last-ditch shot at saving our family; she thought we needed a change of scenery.

It didn't work. A few months later my mother came home to an empty house, my father and the car gone. She called my grandmother, who drove down from Philadelphia to help out. "I helped her buy that car," my grandmother says. "And that dumb son of a bitch stole it. Left her with the motorcycle. Two kids and a fucking motorcycle."

My grandmother once showed me a picture she took of me the day my father left. I'm about two, small and pale, all head and curls, wearing what looks like a girl's shirt and sitting in the open trunk of Grandma's Coupe de Ville, staring at the camera, scared and confused. She asked if I remember the elephant in the trunk. I don't. She said her car had a hydraulic trunk that made a sound like an elephant when it opened and closed. I was beside myself about my father leaving, and she told me if I didn't stop crying, she'd lock me inside with the elephant. I asked if it worked. "You're not crying in the picture, are you?"

Grandma stuck around for a while, even after my mother remarried. My first stepfather, Jay, worked at a Chevy dealership and happened to be the son of a former Phillies outfielder. By all accounts he was a decent man, nice enough, didn't beat her, held a job and worked hard. I think he treated my brother and me well but I can't really say—all I remember about him is that he once gave me a sip of his beer and laughed when I made a face, and that he took me to his dealership to meet Bonecrusher Smith, a local heavyweight who was about to fight Mike Tyson. My first memories are from those years in North Carolina, but that's how they all are, fractured and brief, glimmers of a past life that belonged to somebody else. My mother's face beneath her red beret, stern and proud. Sitting in the backseat of her Camaro with the T-tops off, watching her hair swirl in the wind.

Jay had a son named Josh who was exactly my age. We played on the same T-ball team and took turns getting beaten up by my real brother, who because he was husky hated being called Big Josh. Little Josh was my first and favorite stepsibling, and for the only time in my life I bought the new-brother spiel my mother and stepfather gave me; when they broke up, I would never see him again, and after that I'd know better.

Mom was gone a lot, soldiering, learning Arabic to get promoted faster. Grandma babysat, helped around the house. My brothers and I were latchkey kids, went to school and walked home together and played Atari while we waited for our parents to arrive. Army planes flew over our playground and we feared the Russians. We might have been a normal American family.

My first clear memory is from that time. I was in my room, listening to a record on my toy turntable, when Mom's Camaro rumbled into the driveway. I went into the hall and watched her shadow appear in the curtained window of the door, heard her keys jingle in the lock. Mostly I remember the excitement: Mom was home.

She came in carrying grocery bags, swung them onto the counter, rubbed her hands and sighed. She looked out the window into the backyard while I snuck up behind her, pretending not to see me, just like she pretended not to have heard my jokes so I could tell them again. I threw my arms around her and she jumped in faked surprise, ran her hand through my hair, and said, "How's my baby boy?"

She decided to go to airborne school. She was pushing thirty, raising boys, about to get divorced again. I guess she needed a challenge. She asked Grandma to babysit and went to Georgia, came back a few weeks later, gaunt and haggard, a pair of gleaming wings pinned to her chest.

I once watched her jump out of a plane. Grandma drove us onto post and we sat on bleachers looking out at an empty field. A drone swelled in the distance, like a swarm of bees, and a huge green Hercules came into view, flying low. A door opened and specks began to fall out, their parachutes popping open above them as they settled into a swaying fall. I tried to say a prayer for my mother, because I knew she'd want me to—she stopped and prayed whenever she heard an ambulance, for whatever stranger was hurt—but there were dozens of chutes in the sky and I didn't know which was hers. I concentrated on the distant specks and listened for a message. She said we had a special bond, that one of us would know if the other was in trouble, that we could communicate even when we were far away. I closed my eyes and tried to hear her.

A few months later she missed her drop zone on a botched night jump and landed in a tree, shattered her wrist, hung tangled and in agony for hours before they found her. I hadn't known that she was in pain, didn't get a signal; after that I stopped believing in our secret messages. Later she told me she thought of my brother and me that night, hanging in the tree, trying to distract herself from the pain. She wondered what we were doing at that moment, what we would do without her. She decided not to reenlist.

She and Jay broke up. Nobody remembers whose fault it was. We moved into a gray house at the end of a cul-de-sac. It was quiet, safe, suburban, with a big lawn and a garage, a fireplace and a computer; it's the house I think of when I wonder how our lives might have been if we'd never moved to Tombstone. I learned to ride a bike on the sidewalks of our street, my mother running behind to catch me if I fell.

A middle-aged woman who looked like an older version of my mother lived alone in a brown house next door. A high fence separated our backyards. Josh and I would accidentally throw baseballs and Frisbees into her yard and fight over who had to go get them. I usually lost.

A concrete path split her front yard into two squares of leaf-strewn grass and led to her front door, tucked deep in a dark alcove. I dreaded that walk, felt an eerie danger lurking in that quiet house. Or maybe I didn't; maybe I remember staring at the gold door knocker with a sense of dread only because of what happened later.

When I knocked on her door, our neighbor would answer and smile and let me in, and she'd walk with me through the living room to the backyard, where she'd stand watching as I retrieved the lost ball. She'd offer me something to drink and ask about my mother. She had children, daughters, but I don't remember them.

Right before we moved to Arizona, Josh and I came home from school one day and saw strange cars ringing the cul-de-sac, police cruisers and news vans. When Mom got home, she told us that our neighbor had been hurt, and we prayed for her.

I wouldn't learn the whole story for twenty years, until I searched the local newspaper's archives.*

A month earlier, our neighbor had called the police on her husband after he'd punched her and beaten her head against a wall. One of her daughters told the police that she'd heard her father say to her mother, "I am going to kill you." Our neighbor took her kids out of school and moved into a shelter for domestic violence victims.

She pleaded with the magistrate to prevent her husband from posting bond. She said she feared for her safety. A social worker suggested having him involuntarily committed. The magistrate said it would be a waste of time. The social worker would later tell the newspaper that she saw a look of terror on our neighbor's face.

She filed for divorce and got a restraining order. When her husband called several times a day, parked in our cul-de-sac to watch her, and followed her to a store parking lot, where he begged her to take him back, she reported him. He was served papers to appear in court on charges of contempt.

* "Man Shoots Wife, Self in Cumberland County Grocery Store," *Fayetteville Observer,* May 13, 1988; and "System Failed Shooting Victim," *Fayetteville Observer,* May 15, 1988.

She did everything she could. She did everything right.

On a Thursday morning, our neighbor went to the grocery store with her three-year-old granddaughter. She might not have seen her husband's car behind her, or she might have seen it and decided not to let him control her life anymore. She parked and went inside. He followed her.

A Pepsi vendor making a delivery heard them arguing. Another vendor heard shouting by the soft drinks and turned the corner of the aisle just in time to see the husband draw a pistol—a .25 caliber automatic, the same kind of gun that would later kill my mother. He grabbed his wife and held her as he shot her once in the hand, once in the arm, and finally once in the head. Our neighbor fell. A bullet ricocheted to the front of the store. Customers screamed and ran. Her granddaughter, who watched it all happen, began to cry. The husband held the gun to his head, pulled the trigger, and fell next to his wife. The pistol landed between them. The Pepsi man called the police. A customer led the little girl outside.

The husband died three days later. Our neighbor went into a coma. We moved to Arizona. I once asked my mother what happened to our neighbor, and she said she didn't know, but she often thought of her and wondered, and she often prayed for her. The newspaper says she remained in a coma for eighteen months, then died. Her name was Carolyn.

In the article, a man from the neighborhood says he thought they were friendly people. The article says other neighbors declined to be interviewed, but that's not completely true.

That night my brother and I sat on the floor in the living room, watching on TV as a man with a microphone stood live outside Food Lion. We called out to Mom and told her it was on. She came into the living room just in time to see herself appear on the screen, standing in our front yard that afternoon, with her name in a banner across the bottom, above the word *neighbor*. On-screen, her hair blew in the wind, and standing in the living room hours later, she lifted her hand to fix it.

The reporter held the microphone toward her and she squinted at the neighbor's house, that dark front door, and said they'd seemed so nice, like such normal people. *You just never expect a thing like that to happen*. She'd never been on TV before, and she asked us if that was how she really looked, if that was her real voice. She didn't recognize herself.

WELCOME TO ARIZONA

The town named after Wyatt Earp is way out in the California desert on the Arizona line. I pass through Earp just after sundown, the sky still rosy in the rearview mirror, having spent the last ten hours driving through the dogshit parts of California: Bakersfield, Boron, Barstow, Needles. The lights of RV parks waver on the waters of the Colorado as I coast across the bridge. A sign of a striped sunset welcomes me to Arizona.

I stop at a gas station called Terrible's with a saguaro by its sign and call my friend Ric. It's just past nine on a Tuesday night and he's leaving work. Ric teaches writing at a satellite campus of a junior college here in Parker. He tells me to meet him at a diner down the road in fifteen minutes.

Ric and I were roommates once. We'd both just finished graduate school and were living in Tucson, stringing together part-time jobs. We drove shitty cars that broke down and made us push them along the sweltering streets, ate a lot of eggs, drank cheap beer by the case until we got belligerent and challenged each other to fights. At night we'd sit in the laundry room of our rented house, where we kept our desks, and write short stories. The only mail we got was rejection letters. We joked about how if we ever became famous, we'd look back on that time as our bohemian era.

We meet at the door of the diner, shake hands, and get a table. It's been two years since I've seen Ric. His dark hair is shorter and gray at the temples, his beard better kept, and he has new glasses that are thick-rimmed and sort of hip for a guy who lives in Parker. Otherwise, he looks the same: short and burly, a heavy brow and melancholy eyes, dark and quick. I wonder how I look to him, whether I'm different.

We order eggs and coffee from the waitress and start to catch up. When he asks how I'm doing, it's more of a question than it would be if someone else were asking. The last time we spoke, a couple of months ago, I called him at three a.m. and we talked about depression. It wasn't the first talk like that we've had. We both see a darkness at the edges of our lives, an annihilating sadness; the fact that we can both see it is one reason we're friends.

I say I'm all right and change the subject. His book came out last year, a collection of stories, and I tell him it's great. He thanks me. The waitress comes with our food and a silence sets in as we begin to eat. Ric shakes more salt onto his omelet, slides his silverware along the table, tugs at the front of his Hawaiian shirt. Something's on his mind.

"I read something about you online," he says.

The first result in an Internet search for my name is a brief article from a few months ago, mentioning that I've begun writing a book about my mother's murder.

"You know."

"Yeah." He sets his fork down and wipes his mouth with a

napkin. "I was surprised to read that." He won't make eye contact.

"I'm sorry I never told you. It's just—"

"Sure, no, I understand. Don't apologize."

"I didn't tell anybody." I name a few friends from our Tucson days who also don't know how my mother died. That seems to reassure him.

It's not the first time I've had this conversation. Most of the friends I've made in the last decade are finding out on the Internet that my mother was murdered. I wonder how that feels. It must feel like I didn't trust them enough to tell them. How do I explain that I didn't say it because I knew that if I did, they'd never have thought of me the same again? I would have become the guy they knew whose mom got murdered.

Ric changes the subject, says he wants to hear more about Laura. I tell him the story of how we met, that it's serious, and that we've talked about moving in together in the fall. I don't say the rest of what I'm thinking, that first we've got to make it through this summer. When I left San Francisco, Laura said she understood that this trip was something I had to do, but a lot can change in a few months apart.

Ric says there are other things he wanted to ask. He rummages through his pockets. He writes everything down, posts notes to himself on walls. One he hung above his desk when we were roommates has stuck with me: *Remember the belly of the whale.*

Ric throws up his hands; he's always been sort of theatrical. "I remember what it was," he says. "Why'd you come back?"

It's a question I can't easily answer. Some of the men my mother knew are here. So are the places we lived, and the place where she died. But I don't know why I came back; I only know I had to. This is the belly of the whale.

Ric and I leave the diner and drive out of town on a dark highway into the res. One side of the road is like a scene from an Arizona postcard, a waxing yellow moon above the shadow of a butte. On the other, a giant billboard flashes the name of an Indian casino. Ric parks and we shotgun a few beers in the parking lot. Inside, we find a blackjack table and blow some cash and drink until neither one of us can convince ourselves to drive. Instead we hitch a ride from a bunch of strangers in a lifted pickup, and on the way to Ric's trailer we drink beers in the bed of the truck with a tattooed guy in a backward hat who asks us where we're from. I say Arizona and wonder if it's a lie. As the tires roar on the highway and the wind whips over our heads, I try to imagine what would happen if the drunk guy driving rolled this truck and we all died. Would anybody find the truth in the wreckage? Would anybody try?

But we make it safely to Ric's trailer in a park carved into a desert hillside, where I sleep on the couch and feel strangely nostalgic for Tombstone, the places like this where my family lived. And as I fall asleep I think: *Welcome to Arizona.*

In the morning, on my way out of town, I stop to buy water. In the parking lot of Terrible's, a kid knocks on my car window. He's white, maybe fifteen, shaggy blond hair and acne, swimming in his clothes. He motions for me to roll down the window and asks for change, says he needs gas.

I check my rearview mirror. There aren't any cars at the gas pumps. "Gas for what?"

He shrugs and scratches his elbow. "Just gas, man."

I dig a few quarters out of the console and drop them in his palm. He looks at them and waits a beat like he's expecting more, then turns without a word and walks away stiff-legged, pulling up his shorts. I knew a lot of tweaker kids like him growing up in Tombstone. In a few years he'll be locked up in Florence or withered into a zombie.

The highway outside Parker runs straight and flat through an alkaline wasteland of saltbush and mesquite. Mountains ring the horizon and a gray haze hangs in the sky. It's a hundred degrees, maybe one-ten—I've been gone too long to tell the difference—and the heat makes me realize how much I've missed the desert.

At the edge of Quartzsite a cop car pulls out from behind a blank billboard and follows me through town. I slow down and wait for the red-and-blues. I'm hung over, unshaven, wearing designer sunglasses, and driving a red sports car with California plates; I'm every Arizona cop's wet Taser dream. Empty RV parks pass by, a U-Haul store flying a tattered Stars and Bars. At the turnoff for I-10 the cop drives past, eyeballing me through his aviators. He has a mustache, of course. He reminds me of Ray; cops always do.

Along the highway outside of Phoenix the Joshua trees appear, alone at first and then in bunches. We moved to Arizona when I was six, and I didn't know the names of most things in the desert, couldn't tell a greasewood from a mesquite or a king snake from a coral. But I knew Joshua trees. They're easy to spot, thick greenish limbs covered in thorns that look like golden fur. They were the first desert plant I learned the name of. My mother told me.

The day we first drove into Arizona, she pointed out the window. "Look," she said, "a Joshua tree." She glanced at my brother in the passenger seat. "I love Joshua trees because they're named after you."

Josh stared raptly at the short trees slipping by in the window. He craned his head around his seat, looked at me in the back, and said, "There's no such thing as a Justin tree."

I told him I hated him. I was in a phase of saying that I hated everything. I hated my brother. I hated Arizona, although I'd never been. That morning, leaving the motel in Texas, when she'd said I couldn't sit up front, that it was Josh's turn, I had told my mother that I hated her. "Don't say that to me," she said. "That hurts me." "But I do," I said. "I hate you."

I kicked the back of Josh's seat, said his tree was stupid, and that he couldn't see the particles. Earlier, in some uncharted stretch of west Texas, I'd interrupted a long, dreamlike silence by asking if they saw the circles floating in the air. Mom asked what I meant and I described them. Floaters, she said. She had them, too.

"There aren't any particles," Josh said. "Mom just said that so you'd stop whining."

"Yes, there are," she said. She leaned forward and stared up through the windshield. "If you can see them, it means you have special eyes."

In the backseat I watched her, and when I looked out my window at the sky, I saw them again, circles drifting in the clouds, and I thought that she and I shared the same eyes. "Look," I said. "I can see them. There they are."

I'M NOT HERE

My brother lives near Fort Huachuca, the army base that gave Tombstone its name. In 1887, when Ed Schieffelin left the fort to prospect the hills in Apache country, the soldiers told him all he'd find out there was his tombstone. Instead he found a mother lode of silver, the news of which would later attract the Earp brothers. Now Fort Huachuca is home to the Army Intelligence Center, which teaches interrogation or torture, depending on whom you believe. My mother first came to Arizona because she was sent there for training, but she never said what she learned there. It was one of her secrets.

Josh lives in a tract home development off the highway. Arizona's housing bubble burst in the middle of construction, so entire blocks of the neighborhood are nothing but bull-dozed dirt. The skeletons of a few half-built houses sit exposed and slowly warping. The finished homes are Pueblo-style, flat-roofed and boxy, painted in earth tones and surrounded by small gravel yards. The locals call it Baghdad. Most of the houses on my brother's street are for sale. I can tell which one is his because he takes care of his yard: the gravel is thicker than his neighbors' and the driveway is swept clean.

I ring the doorbell and hear his schnauzer growling inside. Josh opens the door, holding the dog back with his leg. We don't shake hands and we're not huggers; I walk inside and sit on the couch. The Phillies are on TV, playing the Diamondbacks. Josh talks to the dog in a baby voice to calm him down.

"You want the stuff right now?" he asks.

"Sure."

He leads me through the dark alley of the laundry room and into the garage, where he rummages in boxes and stacks objects in my outstretched arms: a white plastic crate and two padded camera bags.

"Is that it?"

"I think so." Josh looks around the garage: an unused mountain bike, a dusty set of golf clubs, a column of empty appliance boxes he insists on keeping, and his white luxury sedan. I wonder how he lives here, an hour's drive from where our mother died, and keeps her things in the garage. I'd be afraid of the past escaping and creeping into the house.

I glance in the crate: a few books, two plastic bags. "What's in here?"

He shrugs. "I don't really know."

We go back inside. I sit on the red leather couch, which makes his otherwise muted living room look like the set of a southwestern porno, and sift through the crate. I open one of the camera bags and remove an old Canon 35 mm. Josh reaches over and picks it up.

"I think this was expensive," he says, unscrewing the lens. He looks into the viewfinder and presses a button on top. "The batteries still work."

Inside the other bag is a video camera. I press the power button, imagining some long-hidden clue to my mother's death that's about to be revealed, a taped statement of Ray's explaining everything, but the battery is dead. The pockets of the bag hold unmarked tapes, a spare battery, and a power cord. I fan the tapes in my hand and ask Josh what's on them. He shrugs again. He's focusing the Canon on the dog, who cocks his head and stares back. We could connect the video camera to his TV and play the tapes right now, but even though he hasn't said it, I know Josh doesn't want any part of this. He has a stable life now, the kind we never knew, a house and a wife and a dog, a career and a retirement plan and life insurance. He's found a place to put the past, and I'm happy for him, but I don't understand how he does it. Doesn't he ever want to walk, to let this life go before something awful comes along and takes it all away? If we were different men, I could ask him.

He watches the Phillies while I rummage through the crate. I find a few books: two volumes from the complete works of Charles Dickens, the *Catechism of the Catholic Church*, and the family Bible, leather bound and worn, its cracked spine patched with packing tape. I open the Bible and papers fall into my lap. A prayer card to Saint Jude, the patron saint of lost causes. A sheet of ruled paper on which my mother wrote passages of Scripture about judgment and forgiveness. *Luke 6:38: "For the measure you give will be the measure you get back."* Another yellowed sheet with a passage from a book called *The Art of Marriage* scrawled in a smaller and more slanted hand than my mother's, which I will later learn to recognize as Ray's. A folded photocopy of a poem called "I'm Not Here," written in rhyming couplets: *Don't stand by my grave and weep / for I'm not there, I do not sleep.*

Mom liked this poem enough to make a copy, and to leave

it in the Bible to be found in case she died; on the back she wrote a note: *I am forever your mother and my love is with you always*. She must have thought the poem would comfort me, but all I see when I read it is a series of saccharine clichés. Maybe if she had learned to recognize clichés, she would have seen that her fantasy of retreating from society to a remote place in the West to live a simpler life was itself a great American cliché, a doomed and foolish pipe dream. Or maybe all the books I've read have made me a snob.

A family register inside the Bible records births and weddings and deaths. The births are current—the last one listed is mine. But the marriage records stop at my mother's first, and the list of deaths is hopelessly outdated.

I put it all back in the crate and we watch the Phillies lose. When the game is over, I say goodbye to my brother, load our mother's things into my car, and leave for Tucson, where I've rented a guesthouse for the summer, and where I'm supposed to meet the man we moved to Arizona with.

THE MAGICIAN

I'm sitting in a Wendy's in South Tucson eating a sandwich I can hardly taste, watching planes descend into the airport, when Brian calls. We were supposed to meet twenty minutes ago. I've been sitting here, having second thoughts, but I make up an excuse. We've been emailing back and forth and talking on the phone for the last few weeks, and I find myself lying to him a lot. I lied about what I do and where I live. He's retired military and a midwesterner, so I didn't want to deal with whatever he'd have pictured if I'd said I'm a writer and I live in San Francisco: pride parades, Communist rallies, Nancy Pelosi. Besides, an unaccountable instinct tells me that when this is over, I won't want him to know where to find me.

I pull into the lot outside Tucson Electric Park, and I spot him standing where he said he'd be, by the ticket booths, in almost the exact spot where I'd camped overnight to buy World Series tickets a month after my mother's death. He's wearing a dark blue shirt with khakis and white running shoes, an outfit he described to me on the phone, but I would have recognized him anyway. For a brief moment I consider stomping on the gas pedal, speeding back to the highway, going home. Instead I pull over and he gets in, says hi, shakes my hand, says it's good to see me. His once-balding head is now completely shaved, and his mustache is now a Fu Manchu, but otherwise he looks about the same. He was older than my mother; she would have been fifty-two this summer, so he must be pushing sixty.

A light rain has just resumed. We talk about the weather as I find a place to park, then walk through the mist toward a white tent stretching across the far end of the parking lot. I ask why he wanted to meet me at the gem show. He doesn't live in Tucson, and he's not a jeweler; he's a part-time magician. He's also into some other business he mentioned on the phone, an opportunity he wanted to talk to me about.

"My business partner is a gemologist," he says. "I'll introduce you."

We walk past a pod of outdoor toilets and through a set of tent flaps. Inside, the tent is busy, at least a hundred people, and most of them seem to be selling something. The air is moist and thick, the light antiseptic. We step across a giant puddle and pass a stall displaying geodes cut in half. The place looks like a field hospital in some geologic war. Brian says the roof has been leaking all day, looks up at the peaked fabric and scowls. "Some tent," he says.

He leads me on a crooked path between racks of beads and turquoise jewelry. The signs above the booths follow no obvious format. Some have a business name, location, and logo—lots of animals and Native or New Age iconography, White Horse Silver from Oklahoma City, Buffalo Spirit from Santa Fe, that sort of thing—but others simply advertise what they sell, Lucite Bracelets and Sterling Silver Jewelry Handmade by

Hopi Indians and chunks of Fordite, which is, according to the man behind the table, layers of automotive paint dried into rock and mined from closed-down factories. Some stalls don't have signs at all. I glance at prices as we pass. We're in the cheap tent.

Brian stops at a stall near the back, beneath a purple sign bearing an indiscriminate reptile, and points to a short, doughy white guy dressed like an undercover cop: a Hawaiian shirt and khakis, a baseball cap pulled low on his head. Brian calls him over and introduces him as his business partner, Doug. Doug's grip is loose and clammy, and although he's much shorter than me, he doesn't look up at my face, choosing instead to stare directly at my chest. Brian says they're partners, but Doug is obviously his sidekick. As they discuss their plans for the evening, it dawns on me that Brian doesn't have his own vehicle. He turns to me and asks where I'm staying, if I want to share a hotel room. I tell him another lie, that I'm staying with a friend; the last thing I want is him crashing on my couch.

Brian tells Doug that I have a car, and volunteers my services as a chauffeur. I ask where we're going.

"We're doing a presentation later at a house in the Foothills," Brian says. "You're coming. I'm going to secure your financial future."

"How's that?"

When he grins, his bald head looks like a skull. "Network marketing."

"OK," I say. Whatever it takes.

He leads me past a group of bored security guards and back out into the parking lot. We stop next to a blue van he says belongs to Doug. They've both by now mentioned the thousands of dollars they make each week from network marketing, and yet Doug drives an old conversion van, windowless and battered, the kind terrorists and pedophiles drive in movies. Brian opens the van's side door, extracts a rolling bag, and hands it to me. I carry it across the lot to my car and dump it in the trunk. He reaches into an outside pocket of the bag and pulls out a thick manila envelope.

"Can't forget this," he says. "This is the stuff about your mom."

He doesn't give it to me; instead, he tucks the envelope under his arm and leads the way back inside the tent.

I found Brian a few weeks ago, before I left California, by searching for him online. I saw a picture and recognized him right away, although before I saw it, I would have had a hard time describing him. He's been cut out of most of our family pictures. I remember doing it, Mom and I, after they broke up. We sat cross-legged on the living room carpet with scissors and a trash bag and snipped. At first it seemed like fun, and we'd show each other the results and giggle as we dumped bits of him into the garbage, but soon a sadness crept over us as we realized it was harder than we thought—traces of him remained, a phantom hand on our shoulders, a stray shoe at the bottom of the frame.

In the email I wrote him, I tried to find the right tone, civil but cool. I said Mom was dead, and that I was trying to find out more about her life, that I wanted to talk to him. He replied the next day: *We will meet and I will help you in your quest.* He gave me his number, told me to call.

I called. We exchanged greetings—awkwardly, but with a strange warmth—and he told me the story of their relationship in a long monologue that seemed rehearsed. "She was the best thing in my life," he said. "And also my greatest heartbreak."

He told me he'd heard about her death a year ago from a friend in the CIA, which he referred to exclusively as "the agency." At first he didn't know that Ray had killed himself. He couldn't find anything about it in the papers.[*] So Brian went back to Tombstone. "I was going to find the son of a bitch and kill him myself."

The Tombstone marshal stonewalled him, so he looked up some old friends and pieced together the story of what happened in the years after he left town. He heard Mom got involved with some shady people. He heard about beatings.

"Beatings?"

"The motorcycle guy," he said.

"What motorcycle guy?"

"My friend in the agency told me about him."

Only later, after we hung up, would I wonder why the CIA would have cared about my mother, or why they wouldn't know that Ray's body had been found. Brian said he'd gone to the Cochise County sheriff and talked to the detective who'd handled the case. He also got the police report. "The complete files," he said. "Except the pictures. I didn't want to see those." He said he had names, Social Security numbers, phone numbers, addresses, everything. I asked him to send it to me. He said he'd do me one better: he was going to Tucson soon for business, and if I met him there, he'd give me the documents and tell me what he knew. He mentioned an opportunity, a company with a vaguely official name.

"The company logo is a Lamborghini," he said, "so you know we're talking big bucks. I'll make you a lot of money."

---

[*] The only news coverage I've found of Ray's death is a brief item from the December 13, 2001, edition of *The Arizona Daily Star,* "Man Sought in Wife's Slaying Is Dead."

In a back corner of the tent, Brian and I find a couple of empty chairs and sit down. Doug disappears down an aisle as Brian begins to tell me how he met my mother. It was in North Carolina, when she was in the army. He was the jumpmaster of her airborne unit. Their marriages fell apart and they started dating; he doesn't say which happened first. She went to Fort Huachuca on a temporary duty assignment and came back raving about how beautiful Arizona was. I don't remember most of what he does, but that part I do: for the rest of her life, when asked why she'd moved to Arizona, my mother would mention that month, say she'd felt at home, as if she'd lived in the desert in some past life. They arranged a transfer.

"I think we were engaged by then," he says. "I don't remember." He looks past me toward the far end of the tent. "Some memories you put away, because you don't want to go back and relive them."

He says we packed our house in North Carolina, rented a truck, and drove across the country. We moved into a Motel 6 in Sierra Vista and they started looking for jobs and a place to live.

"We decided to take a day trip to Tombstone. She said she'd always wanted to see the O.K. Corral." That doesn't sound right; she never seemed to care about the Western myths. It was the land itself that drew her, all that emptiness, something she needed to find. But I don't want to interrupt. Brian's face has relaxed, his eyes focused off in the middle distance; he's found the story.

"And that trip changed our lives."

Wyatt Earp came to Tombstone late in 1879, at the age of thirty-one, searching for a better life. He'd made a reputation for bravery as a lawman in Kansas, but it was dangerous work, and there wasn't any money in it. Tombstone was a remote silver camp in the throes of a breakneck boom. Wyatt arrived with his common-law second wife and his brothers, hoping to go into business. He wanted to start a stagecoach line, but found two already running, so he diversified: filed mining claims, bought real estate, rode shotgun for Wells Fargo, acquired an interest in the faro game at the Oriental Saloon. The Earp brothers cut a wide swath in the infant boomtown. They were young and handsome, ambitious and swaggering; they were outsiders, Yankees, Republicans, lawmen. It didn't take them long to make enemies.

A loose-knit gang of cowboys and outlaws operated on ranches around Tombstone, running and rustling cattle and robbing stages. They were mostly from the South and mostly Democrats, and many had been in the area before the silver boom, so they took exception to the latecomer Earps and the eastern law-and-order interests they represented. A feud began, a series of conflicts over stolen horses, shootings, robberies, political deals gone awry. Still, it might have come to nothing if it weren't for the rumors; the town kept talking about a fight until it got one. On October 26, 1881, in an empty lot behind the O.K. Corral, the Earps and Wyatt's friend Doc Holliday shot it out with the Clantons and McLaurys. Wyatt's party won, or so it seemed at first: they all lived and three of their enemies died in the street.

But Tombstone turned on the Earps. Murder charges were filed, then dismissed. Their political alliances and business interests soured. Two of the Earp brothers were ambushed in revenge, Virgil crippled and Morgan killed, which sent Wyatt on a murderous rampage. Newspapers in California and New York published embroidered stories of the latest lawlessness in the Wild West, while the local media argued over who was to blame. By the time Wyatt finally left Tombstone, two and a half years after he'd arrived, he'd lost a brother, most of his money, many of his friends, and his good name.

Tombstone burned down, was rebuilt, busted. The mines flooded and silver prices tanked. Within a decade the boom years had become a distant memory, and so had the Earps. When Bisbee took the county seat away in 1929, Tombstone had no reason to exist. The town needed a story to survive. It chose Wyatt Earp's.

The first Helldorado, a Western festival timed to roughly commemorate the gunfight, was planned to drum up tourism. The gunfight was reenacted for the first time. The timing was right: a glut of books and movies about the Wild West brought visitors in droves, that year and for decades after. Seventy years after the shootout, a Hollywood movie gave it the name it's been known by ever since: the Gunfight at the O.K. Corral. Now the gunfight happens every day.

When my mother and Brian went to Tombstone that day to see the O.K. Corral, she was about the same age Wyatt had been when he arrived, and like him she was looking to start over. Brian says they were walking up Allen Street when she said she wanted to live there. It was a small town, a good place to raise a family. They could buy a house, maybe start a jewelry store. Brian makes it sound as if he was always a part of her plan, but I have my doubts about that. She knew she could do it alone.

They stopped into a real estate office and struck up a conversation with the owner, Sandra. She and her husband, Tony, would become my mother's first friends in town, and were among the few who stuck with her through the ensuing years; she was managing Tony's restaurant when she met Ray. Sandra had a house for rent on a dead-end street near the elementary school, with a clear view north across the valley all the way to the Dragoon Mountains. When they went to see the house, my mother and Brian stood in the yard looking at the mountains and tried to find the rock formation the locals called Sheep's Head.

They told Sandra they'd think about the house and went to dinner at a steakhouse on Allen Street. As they were eating, the owner, George, came by to say hello. They hit it off, and Brian told him they were getting out of the service and thinking about starting a business.

"You know how quickly I make friends," he tells me.

George asked if they'd ever thought about a restaurant. He took them through a doorway at the back of the steakhouse and into the kitchen, past the steaming dishwashers and the bustling cook line, the humming ice cream maker and the walk-ins clacking shut, through another set of doors until they were standing in another kitchen, bare except for a pizza oven. The former owner had left in the middle of the night and taken everything he could carry, the plates and silverware and glasses, the cash register, the tables and chairs. My mother and Brian wandered through the empty space and imagined what they could build there. They just didn't have the money.

"But George saw the entrepreneurial spirit in us," Brian says. "We were young and vivacious and wanted to change our lives." They struck a deal. They went to Tombstone to see the O.K. Corral, and left with leases on a house and a restaurant.

Brian stops in midsentence, looks over my shoulder, and says, "You found more food."

I turn around to see a beanpole of a man with a bad sunburn

standing behind me eating popcorn. He's wearing a white T-shirt that says "Lemonade," with a picture of a lemon in place of the o. He says he's been carrying a tray of lemonade around all day.

Brian asks how business is going, and Lemonade says he's made a hundred and ninety bucks. Brian perks at the mention of money, and asks what he's going to do with it.

"Hoard it," he says. "I have CDs in the bank."

He's walked right into the trap. Brian tells him he ought to go into business for himself, and launches into an ad hoc analysis of the potential profit margins: the lemonade costs ten cents, the owner charges four dollars, pays him a dollar a cup, and so on. They debate the price of plastic cups, whether they'd be cheaper if you got them from Mexico.

"You're an entrepreneur," Brian says. "I'll teach you how to make money in business."

"I'm an opera singer," Lemonade says.

Brian hardly blinks. "Well, you need to go to Branson."

"I don't do country music."

"They have opera there."

The longer I watch Brian operate, the better I understand his approach. He has an answer for everything. His answers don't make any sense, but it doesn't matter: his game's about projecting authority. He's a confidence man.

Lemonade shoves more popcorn into his mouth. Pieces of it stick to his pink cheeks. "I do epic, heavy metal rock opera," he says.

Even Brian pauses at that. "Well," he says, "it's an entertainment town. . . ."

Lemonade continues. "I do other things, too. Show tunes, whatever. As long as it has good pitch."

Brian doesn't respond for some time, but the lemonade man

sticks around, munching popcorn, surveying his kingdom. Brian invites him to the presentation later tonight, and he shrugs and leaves. Brian asks where he was in the story.

My mother and Brian went to work building the restaurant. They bought equipment and furniture at swap meets, purchased supplies on credit, tried to learn how to make a decent pizza. Brian says they made an agreement: he would work the front of the restaurant, waiting tables, handling the cash, and doing tableside magic tricks. He admits he wasn't very good at magic back then, and would often get caught stuffing handkerchiefs and playing cards up his sleeves, but he says the gimmick was solid gold. Mom would do the cooking. Josh and I would help after school and on the weekends. We decided on a name, drew up a logo of smiling rabbits and a top hat, made T-shirts, hung a sign over the boardwalk, and opened the doors. Pizza Magic was in business.

It didn't take long to see why the last owner had skipped town. Brian says that within a few days of our grand opening, the owner of a restaurant across the street came in and threatened him. We'd unknowingly moved into the middle of a turf war between George, the steakhouse owner who also owned our building, and a group of rival businessmen. Each side had important allies, councilmen and cops. Buildings were vandalized, windows broken, threatening notes left on doors. Rumors started and spread. Tombstone was split into factions, just like it had been with the Earps and Clantons, just like it has been ever since.

We had other problems: Pizza Magic was bleeding money. The location didn't help, on a side street blocks from the main attractions. We tried bringing in a frozen yogurt machine, which infuriated another local businessman, who until then had held a citywide monopoly on the yogurt trade. We bought VHS tapes and started a rental service, but the movies disappeared, and there was no way to collect, because my brother and I had taken most of them. We watched *La Bamba* until the tape wore out.

A carnival came to town for Helldorado. It sucked even by carnival standards, a few sputtering rides and game stalls full of dying goldfish staffed by leering carnies, but we kids loved it. The carnival set up in an empty lot at the end of our street. For a weekend, Pizza Magic was packed.

The day after the carnival left town, a sinkhole opened where the Ferris wheel had been. An old mine stope underneath the surface, one of hundreds like it in Tombstone, had collapsed. The street was cordoned off for months as the city dawdled fixing it. We kept the restaurant open, but nobody came. We wondered if we'd been cursed.

Mom had another idea: movie night. She said the kids in town got into trouble because they were bored, and she thought they'd show up in bunches if we played a movie on a weekend night and sold cheap pizza and soda. I told her the idea was dorky, especially because she wouldn't show *The Lost Boys* like I'd suggested. She picked something PG-13, because she didn't want to get in trouble with any parents. She hadn't figured out yet that most parents in Tombstone didn't give a shit where their kids were or what they were doing, so long as they didn't have to leave the bars to bail them out.

We made signs and posted them on the boardwalk. On movie night the pizzas sat steaming in their trays, pitchers of soda sweating puddles onto the counter. A dozen chairs circled the TV we'd brought from home, all of them empty. My brother and I fiddled with the tracking on the VCR for longer than we needed to, while my mother walked back and forth from the kitchen to the dining room, glancing at the clock.

Brian wasn't there that night; maybe she didn't want to watch him do the same old tricks again. Through the windows, the Pizza Magic sign hung above an empty boardwalk.

Eventually Mom took off the apron, tossed it on the counter, told us to eat and drink as much as we wanted, and went into the kitchen to clean up. She was gone awhile. She'd seen harder times than that, and she must have thought of them: the operating table, my father leaving, hanging tangled in that tree.

To me it seemed like a catastrophe, like we were failing, like *she* was failing. That wasn't true; her and Brian's next idea, to bring in video games and make one of the dining rooms into an arcade, saved the business. But on movie night, for the first time in my life, I doubted her.

Brian keeps talking. I watch people pass by. I haven't been paying attention for a while; it's hard to listen for this long, and the more he says about those years, the more my own memories take over. Doug's baseball cap bobs through the crowd. He arrives and leans into our conversation, pointing to a stall in the middle of the tent.

"See that little guy over there? At the stall for Navajo Dancer?" We nod. "I went to talk to him, and he said it was a pyramid scheme."

"How'd you handle the question?" Brian asks.

"I said I'm a business owner," Doug says indignantly. "That didn't work."

"Did you tell him it doesn't cost anything to look?"

"No." Doug glances again at Navajo Dancer. He tugs at the brim of his hat. "Should we double-team him?" Doug is getting testy. I like him better this way.

"We'll wander over in a minute," Brian says. "Let me finish my story."

Once the street was fixed and the video games arrived, Pizza Magic began to turn a profit. Brian says it was his magic tricks, his knack for attracting customers, but I wonder about that. I remember my mother in the kitchen, covered in sweat and flour, kneading dough and chopping vegetables, sliding pizzas in and out of that furnace-like oven. She worked open to close every day for a couple of years. Only a decade later, when I had a job as a line cook at the steakhouse next door, did I understand what that was like, the suffocating heat, the cuts and burns, dreading each new ticket going up on the wheel, cleaning everything at the end of the night knowing you'd dirty it again in a few hours.

Brian says she left him without warning. He got a line on a job and flew out of state to interview. He thought it would be their ticket out of Tombstone, that they could sell the restaurant and stop having to work those grueling hours. He was gone a week, and when he returned, she'd taken up with another man.

"Just like that?" I ask.

"By the time I came back, there was a restraining order," he says. "She said she was afraid of me."

I don't remember any violence between her and Brian; arguments, sure, raised voices coming from their bedroom, but nothing physical. Brian says the only time he ever laid a hand on her was to lift her onto a counter during an argument to try to calm her down. He says she was the one with the temper, that she'd snap and start throwing dishes or slap him.

That's true about her temper. Once—only once—she hit me. I was about thirteen. We were in the car and I made the kind of wiseass remark she loathed. I didn't see her hand come off the gearshift. She had a ring on and it opened a cut next to my eye. I told her if she ever did that again, I'd break her fucking arm. I didn't mean it, but I said it anyway, because by then I'd seen her get hit enough to know how it worked: if I'd kept quiet and accepted her apology, it would have given her permission to do it again.

Brian says he was stunned when she left him. He hung around Tombstone for a while, trying to get her back, but eventually took the new job and moved. He says he later heard from his friend in the CIA that she'd remarried. "And then the rest of it I learned when I did this," he says. He reaches into his briefcase, pulls out the envelope, and sets it on his lap. He says he spent three days in Tombstone last year, talking to old friends and the police.

I ask for the envelope. He pats it. "Sure," he says. "I'll show it to you later. But I can tell you what happened." He proceeds to tell me his version of my mother's death. She and Ray got into an argument. She rejected him somehow, made a sarcastic comment, impugned his manhood. "I say this very carefully." He lays one hand flat on the envelope and gestures with the other; he's in magician mode, doing a trick. "He didn't have a sense of humor."

"Excuse me?"

"She took every cent I had," he says. "Stole everything that I earned. Destroyed me financially. I had a sense of humor about it. But this other guy, he was a failure at everything he did. When she rejected him, he couldn't handle it. He didn't have a sense of humor."

I clench my teeth and look up at the roof of the tent and resist the urge to snatch the envelope and run.

"Eight bullets is nothing but anger," he continues. "He stood there and he kept pumping in bullets."

"Yeah, I know."

"Eight bullets," he repeats. The detective told me it was

seven bullets, but I don't mention that, because it doesn't really matter. "Do you know what that means?"

"He was angry. I get it."

"That pistol doesn't hold eight bullets. He had to reload."

The gun in question does hold eight bullets, but Brian is convinced that it doesn't. He thinks the investigators botched the case, that there may have been two pistols involved. He wants to know what happened to all the money.

"What money?"

Brian ignores me. He has a theory. He's taken a murder as straightforward as murder can be—the most common murder scenario in America, a man shooting his wife in a fit of rage— and made it into a conspiracy. He says my mother's body had no defensive wounds, although later I'll read the police report and discover that a DNA test of skin taken from her fingernails matched Ray. I've seen this response before, the need to believe it was complicated. In the months after my mother died, before Ray was found, I heard so many theories about her death: drug smugglers, illegal immigrants, terrorists. We don't want to acknowledge how simple murder can be.

"Nobody understands," he says. "You always have to get the truth."

He gets up and says to follow him. As we cross the tent, he continues. "Probably the greatest hurt I've had is your mom getting killed." His bald head bows and shakes from side to side. "Jesus, if there was anything I could have done to make a difference." For a moment, I'm on his side. I know exactly how he feels. Then he repeats what the sheriff supposedly said to him: *Well, she made the wrong choices in life.*

I look away, at the jewelers milling in the pallid light, the displays of semiprecious stones, and I ponder that statement: did the sheriff really say that, or is Brian projecting his own thoughts onto another man? And is it true, is she dead because she made the wrong choices? My mother had bad taste in men, that's for sure, but his line of thinking is just the same old misogyny, victim blaming, the belief that a woman can ask for it. I've heard it before: the rumors after her death, the tone of the questions the cops asked about her past relationships, the Tombstone marshal calling her a black widow, the priest at her funeral mass preaching about penance. It always has to be the woman's fault. And my rage at Brian's words makes me a hypocrite, because sometimes I blame her, too—not Ray, but her—because she chose him in the first place.

But what are the right choices? My mother married the first man she loved, had children, tried to make it work, to do what was expected. He left. After that she raised her kids. It cost her her youth, most of her dreams. It meant that when we were gone she had nobody else, nothing to do, nowhere to go. Men took everything from her, finally her life. Now men blame her for dying.

We might as well blame Wyatt Earp. His legacy leads straight to Ray, right down to the mustache and the badge and the belief that a man solves problems with violence. If it weren't for Wyatt, grown men in Tombstone wouldn't still dress up like gunslingers, as if there weren't any other kinds of men in the frontier West. If it weren't for Wyatt, Tombstone might be known for its silver boom—it was once the largest city between Saint Louis and San Francisco—instead of a thirty-second gunfight that killed three men. If my mother made a wrong choice, it was moving to a town obsessed with Wyatt Earp, where a former deputy would kill her, and other men would say that she deserved it.

Brian stops in front of the booth for Navajo Dancer, where Doug's sales pitch was stymied earlier. The man behind the table ignores us, but Brian looms patiently by a case of pendants until the proprietor relents and says hello.

Brian gives his magician's grin. "My associate tells me you think we're selling a pyramid scheme."

It's not the opening I would have chosen. The proprietor is short and wiry, and the face beneath his black hat is as dark and hard as a roasted nut. He named his business after a tribe that's been cheated and slaughtered by white men for the last few hundred years, and he's from a rural area of New Mexico best known as the old stomping grounds of Billy the Kid. I'd bet he's got a gun somewhere in this stall.

Navajo Dancer stares at Brian for a long time, then frowns and glances at me. I spin a display of necklaces, pretending to be shopping, thinking maybe I'll find something to take back to Laura, but I can't imagine her in anything this tacky. I tell Brian I'll meet him outside.

In my car, on our way to the Foothills for Brian's presentation, he and Doug argue about where to eat. Doug wants to go to a bar and grill near the university; Brian doesn't think we have time.

"They have great burgers," Doug says from the backseat. "I could go for a burger." Brian sits next to me, on the passenger side, fiddling with the radio.

"We can't get a burger in twenty minutes," Brian says.

"We can tell them to be quick."

"It's not physically possible. You can't order and cook and eat a hamburger in twenty minutes."

"We've got forty minutes." In the rearview mirror, Doug checks his watch. "Forty-five."

"We still have to go to Safeway for snacks."

They argue for a while about the snacks. Doug says there are still some veggies and trail mix left over from last night's presentation. Brian says they should get a bottle of wine; he seems to be anticipating a big turnout. Doug says we can't bring wine, because the owner of the house—whom they never mention by name—is in AA. Brian returns to the issue of dinner. Neither of them is willing to budge. Doug has drawn his line in the sand: he wants a hamburger. I decide that I'm with Doug, and will vote for hamburgers if they ask for my opinion, but they don't. Instead, they reach a compromise: we'll get hamburgers, but at McDonald's, which will be faster. They try to tell me how to get to the nearest McDonald's, and begin to argue over that.

"I lived here for seven years," I say. "I know how to get to McDonald's."

The car goes silent as we pass the university, the glowing red letters on the football stadium, the long grassy mall glistening in the rain. The wipers thump across the windshield. Brian eyes the bungalows on his side of the street as if he's wondering what they're worth.

At a red light, without looking at me, he asks what I do these days. "For money, I mean."

His question catches me off guard. I tell the truth, despite myself. "I'm trying to be a writer." It's something I never say, and just as I begin to wonder why I'm being honest, if I expect him to be proud of me, if I want him to, he says:

"Boston Market."

"What?" I look over at him. He's staring out the window at a Boston Market on the corner.

"Maybe that would be good. Look at that line." He taps the window with his finger. "They must be doing something right."

The light turns green. "If you want to go there, tell me now," I say.

We stick with McDonald's. Brian buys value meals for all of us with a credit card. As we eat, he talks about his life after he and Mom broke up, but I don't really listen. After dinner, I follow his directions west down River Road, past strip malls full of art galleries and snowbird restaurants. We turn north on a dark street that leads into the desert. Half a mile later, the city lights behind us drop under the crest of a hill and disappear. Mesquite branches hang over the road. If not for the address signs and gated driveways in the edges of the headlight beams, if not for the strange men in the car with me, this road might remind me of the way I used to take to visit my mother.

Brian directs me down a gravel driveway that ends at a sprawling brick ranch house. As soon as I stop the car, Doug scurries to the front door, and I wind up carrying Brian's briefcase for him. Doug holds the door for us. In the foyer stands a plastic zombie holding a tray half full of candy. At its feet sits a stuffed and mounted dog.

"Jesus Christ."

Doug chuckles. "Oh, it's just a Halloween decoration."

Halloween is months away, but I decide not to ask. Brian leads us through a dark sitting room full of Western furniture: kingly wooden rocking chairs, a tree-trunk coffee table, a shadowy set of bull horns above the door to the backyard. In the next room, a bright kitchen done in Mexican tile, a man and a woman are watching a small television on the counter. They don't seem to notice our presence until Brian introduces me.

"This is my stepson." I give him a look, but he's typing on his BlackBerry. "Well, practically."

Brian says it's almost time for the presentation; we're just waiting for the rest of the people to show up. There's a conference call scheduled that he wants us all to hear. He walks through a doorway into an adjoining dining room to make a phone call. Doug has disappeared down a hallway on the far side of the house. I'm alone with the two strangers. I've already forgotten their names. The man has thick arms and thick glasses, wears a plaid short-sleeved shirt, and paces back and forth across the kitchen; he reminds me of my high school shop teacher. The woman is in her sixties, frail and placid, sitting in a rolling office chair staring raptly at a muted television showing what seems to be an infomercial. The man asks me what I do.

I tell him I'm a writer. They're about to be subjected to enough lies.

"I wrote a book," the woman says. "It's about woodworking." She looks in my direction, finally, but her eyes seem to see something much farther away.

Brian returns and herds us into the living room, saying the conference call is about to start. The woman stays in the kitchen, watching TV. I sit at the far end of a long varnished table, by a window with a view of the city rolling off to the south. A cabinet full of mismatched china and commemorative plates runs the length of the far wall. Doug reappears and takes the chair across from me. A tall, lean stranger in cowboy boots walks into the room and sits, as if he's been here all along, although I've never seen him before and didn't hear him arrive. Brian introduces him as Frank, tells us he's retired air force and a fellow investor in network marketing. The shop teacher slouches in a chair at the far end of the table, between Frank and Brian; the lights in the room seem to focus on him, as if he's waiting to be interrogated. Snacks have been spread across the table, a plastic tray of vegetables and two bowls of trail mix. The bowl between Doug and me is speckled with white yogurt-covered raisins, which I begin to pick out of the bowl and pile onto a napkin in front of me. Doug sees me and starts doing the same. Brian reaches with evident satisfaction for a carrot.

"OK, here we go," Brian says. He presses a button on his

BlackBerry and a female voice, tinny and shrill, comes through the speaker:

> Hello out there across America! This is Pamela Dodge, CEO of National Networks Incorporated! We're glad you could join us to hear more about the amazing opportunities that come with membership in our company!

I scan the faces around me: we're five grown men, sitting at a table, staring at a red cell phone. Pamela Dodge gives way to a man who sounds like an Applebee's waiter: *Hey there! This is John in Wichita, checking in to tell you how network marketing changed my life!* And so on. All told, five different white-sounding voices from midsize cities in the South and Midwest give their testimonials. A former housewife just bought a vacation home in Mexico. A happy couple retired in their forties. Entire broods of children have been sent to the finest colleges our great country of opportunity has to offer. It's the American dream, prerecorded. It lasts exactly ten minutes.

When it ends, Brian brandishes a stack of pamphlets he calls Literature and starts his pitch. It seems like a lot of effort to spend on one person, the guy from the kitchen, who pretends to listen as Brian reads bullet points from the pamphlet. They must have expected more people to show. I reach for the trail mix and catch Doug staring at me as he munches a mouthful of nuts. A smile creeps across his face, and suddenly I realize: they're not just here for the other guy.

Brian asks a series of rhetorical questions—*Do you* want *to be financially secure for the rest of your life?*—and offers escalating dollar amounts he seems to be inventing from whole cloth. Frank chimes in from time to time with a personal anecdote or a stupid joke; he's the good cop. Doug just watches and eats. I could make a run for it, through the living room full of horns and leather, past the ghoulish candy man and the taxidermied dog, out the door and across the driveway to my car. But I wouldn't have the envelope. It's in Brian's briefcase, at his feet.

The presentation drags on for an hour and a half. Brian pulls magazines and contracts out of his bag, draws a diagram to illustrate how much money we'll make in the first month, threatens to play a promotional video on the TV in the kitchen. Doug and I fight for the final raisins in the bowl. Now and then other people arrive at the house and wisely ignore Brian's invitations to join us.

I'm staring out the window, wondering how long this can last, when I smell whiskey. An old woman with orange hair and makeup like drywall spackle sits in the chair next to me. Everyone else ignores her. I stare at the trail mix, hoping she won't strike up a conversation. Under the table, a bony hand caresses my knee. She leans in and says, in what she probably thinks is a whisper: "This is bullshit."

I push my chair back and stand. "I have to go," I say, and make up a lie about staying with a friend, his infant daughter, how I can't go back to his house late. I ask Brian for the envelope. He takes it from his briefcase and says he'll give it to me on the way out; his overnight bag is still in my car. We walk out past the zombie and the dead white dog. Doug follows. The rain has stopped, the clouds have cleared, and the moon has risen full over the desert. I open the trunk to get Brian's bag. When I turn around, he and Doug are standing too close to me.

"So," Brian says, "all we need is two thousand dollars."

"Do you think you can do that?" Doug says.

"No." Saying it satisfies me. "That's too much money."

"You can start with the two-year membership, get your foot in the door," Brian says. "That's only eight hundred."

"Not bad," Doug says.

"I don't have the money." Another lie: I do have the money, what's left of my mother's life insurance. An hour ago, trapped in that dining room, I considered cutting him a check so I could get the envelope and leave and never have to see these people again. But he's not getting my mother's money.

Doug looks to Brian, who seems to be deciding something. "OK. We'll talk more, we have time." I don't know what he means. Once I get my hands on that envelope, we'll never see each other again. I thought he knew that.

Doug shakes my hand and takes the bag inside. Brian reaches into his jacket, pulls out the envelope, and hands it to me. I thank him, and for a moment we stand at arm's reach, and in the light of the moon we look at each other, at who we've both become.

I extend my hand, but he pulls me into a hug instead. His jacket smells like the leather treatment he used to help me break in my first baseball mitt. "It's good to see you," he says into my ear. I pull away. He wishes me luck. "I'm glad you're doing this for your mother," he says. "I loved her very much." He stares off at Mount Lemmon looming black and massive to the north. His eyes look wet, but it's hard to tell. This all seems so scripted, the full moon, the silence, the land stretching soft and silver on every side of us, a goodbye in the desert. The envelope is heavy in my hand. I promise to send it back when I'm done.

A few days later, Brian calls from a conference in Louisville to check in. He wants to see how I'm doing after reading the police reports, and to secure my financial future. I tell him I haven't read the reports yet, which is true; I haven't worked up the nerve. I also tell Brian that I don't have time to do network marketing, but that's a lie. I'm lousy with time. I've spent the days since I saw Brian sitting alone in my rented guesthouse, sweaty and bored, watching Phillies games and talking to Laura on the phone, begging her to come visit. I could attend network marketing conferences, give in-home demonstrations, recruit my friends. But I won't. He had something I needed—information, documents, a side of the story—and I got it. I won. I need to think that I won.

After I say no, his voice loses its shine. "OK," he says. "OK." The sales pitch is over. "Well, I hope you stay in touch. We've still got things to talk about. I'd love to have you come visit sometime."

Beneath the background noise of the convention, I hear something in his voice, a sadness that I recognize. I remember his words at the end of our first phone call: *It's hard for me that it ended up that way.* What he said in that moonlit driveway: *I loved her very much.* I always think the pain of her loss belongs only to me, but he misses her, too, and he has his own regrets. He returned to Arizona after he heard, hoping to find her killer, hoping to understand what happened. I want to hate him for a lot of reasons—because he brought her to Tombstone, and because he was once a father to me and then he wasn't—but I can't, because we're not that different.

I get his address and tell him I'll send back the files. "Some of the old pictures, too. Some of us," I say, although I wonder if there are any left that he hasn't been cut out of.

"That would be nice," he says. "I'd love to see them."

Despite what he says about keeping in touch, I doubt we'll speak again. I realize that what I want to say most is that I'm sorry—sorry for dredging up all this old pain and grief, sorry for cutting his face out of pictures, sorry I'm not going to be part of his network marketing downline. Instead, I tell him to take care and we hang up. That night I dig through the box of my mother's things and find a few pictures of Brian with my brother and me. We're sitting on his shoulders in a pool. We're standing with him on the boardwalk in Tombstone, pointing toy guns at him. We're at a range, taking turns shooting his .380 automatic, the first gun I ever shot. When I look through these old albums now, I see guns everywhere.

I make copies of the pictures and the documents he gave me and mail it all back to him. I don't talk to Brian again, but our last conversation lingers with me: I rejected him and he responded not with anger, like I expected, but with sadness and resignation, just like he handled her rejection years ago. Seeing Brian again only confirmed my hazy childhood memories: he's not a bad man.

But that's what I thought about Ray.

THE CANADIAN

From the front stoop of my rented guesthouse I watch storm clouds roll in from the south. The concrete step beneath me radiates the heat of the day, and a warm breeze blows ribbons of dust through the streets. The guesthouse is an old adobe with no air-conditioning, four tiny rooms of stifling heat. I sublet it for the summer from a graduate student studying archaeology, and the walls are hung with wooden masks and paintings of dark and faceless figures. Now my mother's last effects sit in a crate on the living room floor, and the police report of her murder lies unread on the coffee table. I try not to spend much time inside.

It's monsoon season. Brooding clouds have gathered the last few evenings, and each time I've sat here waiting for rain that hasn't come. Thunder rumbles. Maybe tonight.

Inside, the phone rings. I hurry to get it; I'm expecting a call.

"Justin." It's him. His voice is low and raspy, not the bellow I remember, and he sounds older. But it's definitely him.

"Max." It's been a long time since I've said his name, felt this sibilant hiss in my teeth. A long breath escapes me. "Thanks for calling me back."

"I'm sorry about your mother."

There are a lot of things Max could be sorry about, but he means he's sorry that she's dead.

"You heard."

"Yes."

"The whole story?"

"Bits and pieces."

I give him the condensed version.

"Good Lord," he says. There's a long pause, and then his voice lifts: "So how are you doing?"

We talk about our lives. He's remarried and owns a business. He updates me on his sons, the twins who were my stepsiblings. He asks about my brother and me, and I tell him Josh is married and I'm about to move in with my girlfriend. We talk mostly about women. He says he's often wondered where we are and how we're doing. Soon we run out of things to say. He suggests lunch, and we set up a time.

I hang up and go back outside to watch the storm. Max was nice on the phone; I don't know why I expected otherwise. We hated each other for most of the time they were married, but what does that mean? I was a shithead kid, adolescent and fatherless, and he came along and married her and stuck around longer than anybody else had, so the task of being the evil stepdad fell to him. I hated him mostly because he was there, although he gave me other reasons.

The storm rumbles and glowers for a while, but soon it blows over.

133

Once Brian was gone, Mom didn't waste any time: she sold the pizza place and bought a gift shop named Madame Mustache, after a brothel owner from the boomtown era, across the street from where Morgan Earp was killed. We moved into a trailer a few miles outside of Tombstone. It was the first trailer we lived in, but it was nice as trailers go, a three-bedroom double-wide in a neighborhood called Holiday Ranch Estates, which locals called Holiday because it didn't deserve such a fancy name. Holiday was outside the city limits, with no zoning laws or organizing logic; our trailer sat across the street from a six-bedroom mansion. There weren't any laws against owning livestock, so my mother bought a couple of horses and went riding every day. She took me with her a few times. I hated horses—still do—how stupid and slow and skittish they are, how much of a pain in the ass: all that shit to shovel, all that hay to stack. I wanted a dirt bike.

Then she married Bill, the other man Brian mentioned, a tourist from Washington, D.C., she'd met at Pizza Magic. Bill and his two sons moved in with us. Bill was my grandparents' age, and I said as much once, during a car ride early in their relationship, after which my mother scolded me. Bill was also rich. He had a pool built in the backyard to win us over, and took us along to Hawaii on their honeymoon, ten days with the whole family in paradise. Mom let me pack my own luggage, and I tried to take my cap gun on the plane in my carry-on, creating a situation at the X-ray scanner. We had to ship it separately, or that's what Mom said when she came back from the security room—I never saw that gun again. In Hawaii we went snorkeling and took a helicopter ride. Six months later they got divorced.

Mom was single for a while. We moved into an adobe shot-gun shack in Tombstone proper that she'd bought for sixteen thousand dollars. It had holes in the roof and peeling paint and mouse shit caked in the cupboards, no air-conditioning and no heat. During the winter she left the oven on at night to give off a dim orange glow and the suggestion of warmth. She called it a fixer-upper. It was the worst place we ever lived, but I loved it like no other, because for a brief while there were no men around, just Mom and Josh and me.

It didn't last long. One day she mentioned that she was going on a date with a man who owned a T-shirt printing shop in Sierra Vista, one of Madame Mustache's suppliers. I was sitting in the living room that night, watching *MacGyver,* when I heard a car rumble into the driveway and looked out the window to see a long white Cadillac beaming its head-lights through the cacti in our front yard. Mom came out of her bedroom wearing a dress, makeup, and dangly earrings. When she kissed my cheek to say goodbye, I smelled perfume. I watched through the window as she walked out and climbed into the Cadillac, and I got my first glimpse of Max in the dome light before she closed the door: a big round head with silver hair and a dark mustache. Later I would wonder if he saw me there in the window, staring suspiciously out at him, and if that moment made us enemies.

Their relationship moved quickly; hers always did. A few months later we sold our adobe and moved twenty miles away, into his sprawling house in a subdivision outside Sierra Vista called Country Club Estates. The houses there had green lawns and big garages, backyards bordering fairways and ponds, ex-otic cars in the driveways: one of the neighbors had two Porsche 911s, a fact I noted with astonishment on our first trip there. For the rest of the brief time we lived in that neighborhood, I watched the front door of that house every time we passed it, hoping to catch a glimpse of the person important enough to own two different Porsches.

Max's house had four bedrooms, a garage, a pool, a Soloflex, a computer, and a dog, a chocolate lab named Buck who chased tennis balls. He also had twin teenage boys, two years older than Josh, who drove an old truck they'd fixed up themselves, played varsity football, and were about to leave for college. They were sometimes nice to me and always tolerant, which was more than I could say for my real brother at the time, so I tried to think of them as brothers, but it never really stuck. Then Max's T-shirt shop went under. He sold his house, and we moved back to Tombstone.

The movie *Tombstone* had begun shooting in the area by then, and it was the biggest thing to happen to the town in decades. Kurt Russell came into Madame Mustache one day, and a guy who'd worked for us got a bit part as a barber, even spoke a line during the scene when Doc Holliday braces Johnny Ringo in the street. There were rumors that Kevin Costner would play Wyatt Earp in another movie. Tombstone was going to be famous again.

Dozens of movies about the Earps had already been made. Wyatt himself hung around Hollywood in the early years of Westerns—a young John Wayne met him on a movie set, and later claimed to have based his laconic lawman characters on Wyatt—and everyone from Errol Flynn to Henry Fonda to Ronald Reagan played him on the silver screen. But the recent decline of the Western genre had been a bad omen for Tombstone, which depended on tourism for its survival. Like every other shopkeeper on Allen Street, Mom and Max hoped the new movies would bring in business.

They decided to branch out. With the profits from Madame Mustache, they bought a cavernous two-story building at the other end of Allen Street that had a run-down gift shop on the first floor and an apartment on the second, with a long weed-choked alley in back where Max could park his boat and RV.

We went to work again, just like we had with Brian, a different family building a different business. We renovated the apartment upstairs and turned the downstairs into two storefronts. One was a gift shop; the other was a paradise to my sixth-grade sensibilities, an old-time ice cream parlor replete with twelve flavors of ice cream and an antique soda counter we'd bought from a bankrupt restaurant in Bisbee and hauled over in Max's pickup truck. The twins and Max did most of the heavy work; Josh and Mom and I did a lot of cleaning and painting. I wrote swear words on the closet ceilings for future residents to discover. We kept the building's longtime name: the Silver Nugget. Next we renovated Madame Mustache, brought in a fudge-making machine and converted the back of the store into an old-time photo studio. The sign painter, the same guy who'd played the barber in *Tombstone*, misspelled it as an "Old Thyme Photo Studio." When I pointed out the error, Mom told me to stop being such a snot.

By the time we finished, we had a retail presence on Allen Street that rivaled anybody in town, and the same businessmen who'd once thought of my mother and Brian as an annoyance now hated her and Max. She didn't care. Neither did I. Walking down the boardwalk between our businesses, it felt like we owned the town.

Our domestic life was less triumphant. Max and Mom spent every minute together, at work and at home—it was beginning to seem like a pattern with her—and it didn't take long for the cracks to show. Josh and I drove Max nuts by bitching and moaning about the work we had to do, and Mom was often forced to intervene. Soon I began to hear them through my bedroom walls, shouting at each other.

I began to truly hate Max during the World Series. The Phillies had won the pennant after eons of futility, and earned the right to play Toronto, the defending champions. Josh and I were ecstatic; even though we hadn't lived in Philly for years, we still loved the Phils, knew all the players, even the reserves. I wore Lenny Dykstra's number four in Little League, and once named a dog Dutch, after Darren Daulton, the Phillies catcher.

Max was Canadian. When Joe Carter hit the series-winning homer for Toronto in game six, he started whooping and carrying on in the living room. Josh and I went to our rooms and slammed the doors behind us as the fireworks boomed on the TV.

Around that time my dad called Mom and said he was moving to Arizona. It was the latest in a series of short-lived symbolic gestures he had made toward being a better father. A couple of years after he and my mother divorced, when we were living in North Carolina, he'd decided to sue for custody of my brother and me, probably as a way of avoiding the child support he rarely paid. He lost, of course, and we didn't hear from him for a few years after that. But when we moved to Tombstone he tried to patch things up, called every couple of months, even flew me out to New Hampshire one summer to visit. Once I was there, he tried to convince me to stay, and forced me to call my mother and ask if I could. She told me to put him on the phone. I heard her screaming at him and watched my father flinch and fidget until they hung up. I flew home the next day. Nobody ever mentioned it again.

One night when my mother came to tuck me in, she sat on

the edge of my water bed and said she had something to tell me. I put down the book I was reading, one of the Westerns she'd bought me at Walmart.

"I talked to your father today," she said. She wouldn't look at me. "He might be coming out here."

"When?"

"He doesn't know. He needs to save some money."

"Give him some."

She squeezed my arm, too hard. "He asked me to. I said no."

I badgered her about it for a while. Finally she said, "You have a savings account. Why don't you loan him the money?"

She must have thought that would shut me up, but it didn't. "How much does he want?"

"Three hundred."

"How much do I have?"

"About three-fifty."

I'd been saving for a dirt bike for the last year. I banked my Christmas and birthday checks, my allowance, the money she gave me for doing odd jobs at the gift shops. But she wasn't ever going to let me have a dirt bike, because she knew I'd only hurt myself, and I guess she wanted to teach me something about my father, a lesson I'd have to learn sometime.

"Will he pay it back?"

She traced a scratch in the bed rail with her finger. "I don't know."

I thought about it for a little while.

"Do you think I should?"

"No."

Max's steps thumped in the hallway. I knew my mother still loved my father—she cried every year on their anniversary—and I thought that if he moved to Arizona, Max might disappear. I told her to send him a check.

We said goodnight. She left the light on so I could read, but told me not to stay up too late. Walking away, down the hall, she must have known how it would go. My father wouldn't pay me back, and he wouldn't move to Arizona, and they certainly wouldn't get back together. We'd stop hearing from him again, and she'd take the blame, and for years I'd bring up the dirt bike every time she asked me to do a chore.

But at least I'd learn not to depend on my father.

I don't remember the first time Max hit my mother, only the way it felt to know that it had happened, the silence and the dread, like being on a spaceship and watching the Earth explode. I don't remember how many times it happened; in my memory they've combined into one long beating. He slapped her, threw her into walls, and once, when she stuck her finger in his face, he bit it to the bone. He liked to do it in the kitchen, or maybe those were just the times I saw. At first she'd call the cops, and he'd get hauled off to jail, but she never pressed charges and she always took him back, and after a while she ended the charade of calling.

I started scheming ways to kill him: rat poison in his whiskey, cutting the brake lines of his truck. It was my version of counting sheep. In one fantasy, I imagined sneaking through the door, creeping to the gun case, grabbing one of the shotguns, and walking to his side of the bed. I'd make sure to wake him up before I pulled the trigger, so he would know that it was me.

My brother and I told our mother every night how much we hated Max, and he'd already abused her more than once, but she married him anyway. They came home from a trip to Vegas and stood in the kitchen digging our souvenir gifts out of plastic bags, and as she handed mine to me, I saw the ring on her finger and burst out crying. She followed me into my room and swore it was a spontaneous decision, as if that made it any better. She tried to lay a guilt trip on me by saying that Max's sons had congratulated them. I told her I was leaving and rode my bike to my best friend Danny's house.

Danny didn't have a dad—none of my friends did—but he didn't have a stepdad either, just an old alcoholic mom who doted on me because she knew I had troubles at home, a phrase that would become a refrain, in detention and in the principal's office and eventually in a courtroom. Danny's mom would sit me down on the plastic-wrapped sofa in her dim and smoky living room and tell me about the fifth dimension, where our souls go when we die, and where there is no pain, and I would pretend to listen and smell the booze on her breath with curious relish, and after she went to bed Danny and I would fill a plastic cup with her cheap Scotch and slug it down. I stayed at Danny's for a few days without calling and then came home, and Mom made a big fuss over me for about an hour, and then everything was the same again.

Later, Max hit my brother in the head with a tennis racket. I wasn't there for that, but Max denied only the details: he said he hit him with the strings, not the metal frame, and that it was just a whack. The knot on Josh's head said something else. Mom made a big show of dialing 911, and later my brother and I went out to the balcony and watched a Tombstone deputy load Max into the back of a squad car. Mom lingered on the boardwalk below us, thanking the cop. As the car pulled away, Mom stepped down into the street, arms crossed, tears glistening on her face in the streetlight, and watched until it turned the corner.

"I bet you she takes him back," I said.

"No way," Josh said. "Not this time."

Sure enough, Max showed up the next day, croaking and

rubbing his throat, saying he'd spent the night in the Bisbee jail getting beaten up by Mexicans and that they wouldn't give him water the whole time. Mom had vast reserves of pity, and he tapped them like a baron; it would take years for him to bleed her dry. We had a family meeting where they fed us some story about Max having a chemical imbalance and a medication that would change him.

I figured I was next. I started hiding under my water bed, in a dark and narrow crawl space that fit me like a coffin and had a door I could close behind me. Whenever I was home with Max and Mom wasn't there, I'd take a bag of candy, a flashlight, and one of the books my mother bought me, and I'd hide in the crawl space for hours, forgetting where and who I was as I read about exotic worlds and adventure, hoping Max wouldn't find me and hassle me to do chores.

One day I was down there reading *Robinson Crusoe* when I heard a knock inches from my head. I turned off the flashlight and slid down deeper into the dark. Another knock. I held my breath. Finally the door opened and I saw Max's big veiny hand, gesturing.

"Come on out."

I pulled myself through the opening, noticing with a pang that my shoulders were getting too big to clear its edges. Max said he had something for me to do outside. I followed him for a few steps, but I didn't want to go sand the wood on the boat, or wash the RV, or unload whatever was in the back of his truck. I was sick of the Cinderella shit. I wanted to lie in the dark and eat Starburst.

"I'm busy," I said.

Max wheeled around and glared at me. "What did you say?"

"I said I'm busy. Leave me alone."

His face flushed and he took a step toward me. I thought: this is it. He'd never laid a hand on me, and I wanted to get it over with. His eyebrows twitched and his fists opened and closed. He was thinking about it. Instead he grabbed a Nintendo controller off of my dresser and threw it at me, missing badly, then stormed out of my room. I stood there for a while, fighting down the same feeling I'd come to recognize, a mixture of nausea and excitement at the prospect of violence— hollow stomach, pounding heart. I didn't do the chore.

It was the first time he let me think that I had won. After that I pushed him further, tried harder to turn Mom against him. Later I'd look back on that moment as the turning point in the war, the day I finally fought back.

Max and I arrange to meet at a bar and grill in an upscale strip mall near the university. I walk in the back entrance and circle a bank of high tables by the bar, casing the booths in the dining area, looking for him. He spots me first: when I see him, he's already leaning forward, pointing a finger at me and smiling. Steven, one of the twins, sits with him in a corner booth big enough for an entire family. I pass an exit on the way to his table and imagine walking through it.

Instead I slide into the booth, say hello, shake their hands. There's an awkward pause as we pick up menus and a too-attentive waiter appears to take our drink order. The restaurant is new, another stylish and overpriced joint with misters on the patio and frigid air-conditioning, painted in earth tones and lit in soft gold hues, built for snowbirds who want to pretend they're in Scottsdale. I've driven by a dozen times but never been inside. I scan the menu and wonder who's paying.

Max asks how I've been.

"Good. You?"

"Good." He nods. We both look at Steven.

"I'm good."

"Everyone's good," Max says. "Business is good. Life is good." For a moment I wonder if he's gone positive on me, become a born-again Christian or joined a network marketing business. Maybe he's just happy.

"It's good to see you," I say. It's not, but this is already going better than I thought it would all those times I imagined seeing him again. We're not squaring off at twenty paces in a dusty street.

It's been fifteen years since I last saw him, and he looks a little older, his hair a little whiter, his face looser in the jowls, but otherwise he's the same guy, the same black mustache and quick, toothless smile, handsome and bronzed, like a Boca gigolo. Steven is a younger version of his father, about thirty-five now, tall and thick-chested, with curly black hair and a deep reddish tan, but he's quieter than Max, quick-eyed and polite and not much of a talker. Three large men with heavy brows and giant heads; the waiter probably thinks we're a family. I resemble Max more than I do my real father, or any of my other stepdads, and I guess it fits: I lived with him for longer than the others. He's the closest thing to a father that I ever had.

We talk about old times. He asks if I remember the trip to Lake Havasu.

The summer before his twins left for college, we loaded the RV and hitched the boat and took a long family trip through Arizona, to Lake Mead and Lake Havasu, finally to Vegas. On a boat trip we got caught miles from harbor in a monsoon that swallowed the horizon in purple bands of rain and dumped torrents on our bare heads, whipped the lake into whitecaps, nearly sank us. The boat broke and I helped Max try to fix it, fetching tools without complaining, for once, and Josh grabbed my arm, gave me a pained look, and hissed, "What are you, *friends* now?" Later, the brakes on the RV failed going down a steep hill and we barreled through a busy intersection with Max laying on the horn and shouting from the driver's seat to grab hold of something, but somehow guiding us through. We stayed at a trailer park in downtown Vegas, miles off the Strip, and I woke up on the floor of the RV to find it shaking because they were having sex in the bed above the front seats, so I got up and stole money from his wallet to use in the slot machines. Sure, Max, I remember.

"Remember the time the car wouldn't shift?"

"No."

"The Jetta."

I remember the car, a boxy beige relic with a circle burned into the dashboard from when Mom made me wait in the car while she ran into a store, even though she knew I hated that, and I heated up the cigarette lighter and pushed it into the plastic. But I don't remember taking it to Havasu.

"The transmission went out. We lost first gear." Max's eyes drift to the ceiling and lose focus. "I couldn't slow down too much or it would stall. Your mother and I got it push-started, and we drove in circles around the campground"—he draws loops on the table with his finger—"and you guys jumped in while it was moving. We drove to the dealership and blew straight through the entrance and into the garage, and I got out and threw the guy the keys and said, 'Fix it, I'll be back tomorrow.'" He claps his hands, then spreads them apart: the end. He always did know how to tell a story.

Max chuckles. He likes that memory. I don't remember it, but that doesn't mean it didn't happen. Everyone I talk to about my mother has these anecdotes. When they want to remember her, they pull them out and dust them off, and they say: that was us, that's how it was. His truth isn't wrong—we were a makeshift family, always on the move, always broken and trying to invent a fix—but it is selective. My memories are different. They involve the kitchen counter, shouts and bruises and blood, police lights wheeling in my bedroom window, and the time in the living room when he told me he was never leaving, and I asked if we'd have to kill him, and he said yes, and I said OK. My version of the truth is just as selective as his; it leaves out all the good times, and there were some. But I believe mine.

After a couple of years, we sold the Silver Nugget. Max's sons had gone away to college, and Josh would follow in a year, so we didn't need all that space anymore, and my mother was sick of the businesses running her ragged. She was restless again. She and Max bought a piece of land out in the farthest reaches of Holiday, just down the road from where we'd lived in the trailer with the pool. It was five acres of unimproved hillside, no buildings and no utilities, on a crooked dirt road named after Fred White, the Tombstone marshal killed by Curly Bill Brocious in one of the events leading up to the O.K. Corral.

The land became Mom and Max's last project. They put us to work again: Max ran the backhoe, digging trenches for utilities and grading a driveway, yanking sticks and grinding gears and shouting orders. My mother, my brother, and I did the shit work, shoveling dirt and driving fence posts and hauling rocks from the wash to line the driveway. I ate a lot of silent sunburned lunches that summer, sitting on the backhoe blade, wishing I had different parents and lived somewhere else. By the fall we'd achieved my family's version of the American dream: a brand-new double-wide trailer set atop a hill, with horse corrals and a hay barn and a clear view north across a thousand square miles of government land to Sheep's Head Mountain.

Max didn't stick around long enough to unpack. By then

they were fighting constantly, about work and about money and about me. I was becoming a problem, the last kid left and a bad one at that, always in trouble at school, constantly provoking Max to drive a wedge between them. Our family dinners, which until recently had been lavish spreads for six people—years later, when I asked why she stayed with Max for so long, my mother would mention those dinners, how it had felt like we were a real family for once—became tense and meager, frozen lasagna and a head of iceberg drenched in ranch, scraping forks and clinking cups and pregnant pauses, fat yellow moths thumping against the windows. Max's back had gone out on him while we were working on the property, and he spent days lying in bed with his legs propped up on pillows. He didn't ride horses, and Mom had sold hers after she met him, but now she bought two more, and started taking long rides through the desert alone, making up for lost time.

After a few months in the new place, I came home from middle school baseball practice to find my prayers answered, Max gone, all signs of his presence erased. Mom sat me down and told me through a veil of pain that he had left. She said he'd tried to hit her again, but I didn't know what that meant, why he would have had to try after so much practice. I'd finally won, finally gotten rid of him, but sitting in that strange and new-smelling trailer with my mother sobbing quietly, it didn't feel like much of a victory. She'd just finally gotten sick of the abuse, not so much the pain itself—she'd known worse—but the shame, the struggle, me never shutting up about how much I hated him.

Max took the RV and moved into a trailer park off a freeway exit in Tucson. Mom would visit him a few times a month. Max had taken his dog, Buck, with him when he left, and I missed that dog. I walked Buck along the banks of the bone-dry Santa Cruz, throwing tennis balls into clumps of saltbush for Buck to fetch and watching the sun set over the hump of Sentinel Peak, listening to the whisk of traffic on the interstate and wondering if they really thought I was too stupid to understand why they'd send me out to walk the dog. I had a moment of terror when she raised the possibility of them getting back together, but soon they went cold turkey.

Our food arrives. I pick at my club sandwich and ask after Max's health. In response, he rolls up the leg of his Bermuda shorts to reveal a thin scar running vertically through his kneecap.

"Replacement knees," he says, patting his fake patella. "Just had both of them done." He says all those years of hockey as a kid in Canada finally caught up with him. He says he's mostly recovered from the surgeries, but it's still hard to ride his motorcycle. He has a Harley now. I remember Brian's words: the motorcycle guy.

"That's how I heard about your mum," he says. When he mentions her, he looks down at the table. Steven looks away, toward the bar. I sip my drink and wait out the silence. Max tells me he went to Tombstone on a trip with some motorcycle friends a few years ago. They stopped in the saloon by Madame Mustache and Max mentioned to the waitress that he used to own the place next door. She asked if he knew Debbie. He said she'd been his wife. The waitress said she was sorry.

"I knew right then," he says. "She told me the story, and I nearly fell over."

"We wanted to tell you," I say. "We didn't know how to get in touch. . . ." But I trail off, because it's a lie—we didn't try to get in touch with him, or any of her other exes. We didn't even discuss it.

"The last time I talked to her was on the phone," Max says. "You'd been in an accident."

Riding in a friend's SUV during lunch my freshman year of high school, with five other kids sandwiched in the seats, on our way to eat tamales somebody's mother had made, I felt a rumble through the floor as the tires hit the gravel shoulder of the road. The tires screeched, followed by an awful quiet as the world tilted in the windows, then screams and blackness. Waking up in the backseat seconds later was like being born into a new world of shattered glass and steel and bone, a throb growing in my neck, a classmate in the front seat with his face a wall of blood, screaming for an ambulance, another lying facedown in the road. Candida: an hour earlier we'd been sitting in keyboarding class, slipping folded notes across our desks to make each other laugh. I climbed out the broken window and went to her. A stream of blood escaped her chest and ran downhill, back toward town. She took a breath—later the doctors would tell me it was impossible, that she had died instantly, but I saw it—and then went still. I knelt down next to her and said her name. The asphalt was so hot I worried it would burn her. A car came around the bend and I ran down the road to stop it. I wound up in somebody's pickup truck, bleeding onto the upholstery, with a Tombstone cop telling me how lucky I was as the paramedics laid a sheet over Candida. Mom was in Mexico, vacationing with the doctor she was seeing. She and Max had been broken up for at least a year by then.

"She called you?"

"She was shaken up real bad. She wanted somebody to talk to."

But him? It strikes me again how poorly I understood what our way of life was like for her. If I needed something—lunch money, girl advice—I went to her. But when she needed someone, who did she have? She couldn't talk to me about her problems, and I wouldn't have listened if she'd tried. Her parents were three thousand miles away, and with all the drugs he did, her brother might as well have been. Work and kids kept her from making many friends; she didn't have the time or inclination to go out to the bars on Allen Street, the only social scene in Tombstone, where the locals gossiped and drank. She had too many strikes against her in the eyes of the town: she was an outsider, she was successful, she went through a lot of men, and she wasn't an alcoholic. She was the worst thing you can be in Tombstone: *too good*. She called Max because she was lonely, and because she'd always trusted him, even after he'd proved that she shouldn't.

Max says business is good, that he's making a living even after the bust. He says he's remarried and happy, but I already know that. A week ago I went down to the county courthouse and ran a records check on Max to see what he's been up to these last fifteen years. When I saw that he'd married again, I checked for domestic violence arrests and found nothing. Maybe he changed, or maybe she doesn't call the cops.

Soon our food has been eaten and our plates are cleared, and we're stumbling through silences and talking about cars. We've been here for an hour and we're boring one another already. The waiter brings the check and I offer to pay, but Max waves me off, as I knew he would; even if he were dead broke, he'd still want to meet in a place like this, and he'd insist on paying. In the ensuing silence we check our watches and press our palms against the table and get up slowly. Outside we linger in the nuclear sunlight of an Arizona summer and shake hands repeatedly and lie about keeping in touch. I'm running out of time, just seconds now, and nothing has been done. I dreamed for years about this moment, when I'd have grown bigger and stronger than him, and I'd have the power to avenge her. But Max is almost seventy now—he just told me he has grandkids—and what am I supposed to do, punch an old man with plastic knees in a parking lot? She never would have wanted me to become a violent man. And it's hard to think of it as revenge when he's not the man who killed her.

THE DETECTIVE

The Cochise County Courthouse sits at the top of a winding canyon road in Bisbee, its five-story façade tinted pink in the afternoon light. Bisbee stole the county seat eighty years ago, but Tombstone still has the better courthouse, a sensible brick Victorian with a courtroom and a jail and a gallows yard. Bisbee went Art Deco: polished copper doors, a tympanum of two kneeling miners, and a statue of a shirtless man in the parking lot, dedicated to "those virile men, the copper miners."

I climb two flights of steps and enter the building's copper maw into a dim foyer, where I explain to the security guard that I'm here to request public records. He makes me empty my pockets and walk through a metal detector. As I'm reclaiming my keys from the bin, something in the pink-and-turquoise lobby sparks a memory: the last time I was here, I was a defendant, and my mother was with me.

After Max left, I took advantage of my newfound freedom and became a teenage delinquent. It started with small-time shenanigans, shoplifting from the stores uptown and giving tourists bad directions, but soon it escalated into cutting school, stealing Scotch and cigarettes from Danny's mother, and drinking in the ditch out back of his apartment building.

Danny got a pellet gun for Christmas. It was a terrible gift. All my friends had BB guns, but this was something else entirely, an awesome piece of weaponry for a thirteen-year-old boy to own: semiautomatic, CO_2-powered, capable of shooting savage pointed-tip lead pellets at over a thousand feet per second.

We hunted after school. First we shot at birds, then jackrabbits, then any dog that had ever chased us. We killed a few birds and a rabbit or two, but the rush it gave us never lasted long, and we wanted bigger prey. We graduated to hiding in bushes by the road and taking potshots at passing cars. It was only a matter of time until we shot a person, though I assumed it would be each other.

One day after school, Danny and I stomped through the bushes in the empty lot by his apartment building. We spotted one of our classmates walking up the street in our direction. Samantha: a tall girl, blond and quiet, whom we rarely noticed except to tease her about her height. She was with her little sister and a friend. Danny hatched a plan: I would hang out in the empty lot, acting casual, distracting the girls while Danny crept through the bushes toward them. When he got close enough, he'd pop up with the gun and scare them.

The plan went south. I overplayed my part, stuck my hands in my pockets and kicked at rocks, might as well have started whistling. The girls spotted Danny fumbling through the brush and asked what the hell he was doing. But Danny stood up anyway and pointed the gun.

Samantha laughed. "You wouldn't do it, Danny. You're too much of a pussy."

Danny went to the nurse's office every day to take a pill that kept him calm. In other places he might have been diagnosed with a condition, something with an acronym, but in Tombstone he was hyper. From across the lot I saw his face flush red and knew he was going to shoot them, and in that moment a strange feeling filled me, partly dread and partly glee and partly admiration. I didn't try to stop him; I just stood there, gaping, as he pulled the trigger. A crack rang off the apartment walls. Samantha cried out in pain and doubled over, grabbing her leg. Danny paused, and I hoped he was done shooting, because I'd already lost the stomach for it. But he fired again, and again and again and again, a volley of shots that came so fast they shared a sound. A scream, another. When it was over, all three girls had been hit and were grabbing at their tiny wounds, crying.

Danny snapped out of his trance and stared at the gun in his hands for a second, then dropped it and ran toward the girls, shouting about how sorry he was. They swore and slapped him. I stood in the empty lot and watched.

Mom was gone somewhere. She might have been with one of her post-Max boyfriends, or she might have been out flying; after Max left, she'd begun taking lessons to get her pilot's license, said it had always been a dream of hers. All I know is that she wasn't home when the police car dropped me off.

But she heard. Did she ever. I'd seen her angry plenty, but never quite like this. I held the phone at arm's length and listened as she called me a coward and a disgrace. She said she was taking away all of my weapons, my pocket knives and sling-shot and BB gun, and she grounded me for a year, although we both knew she wouldn't be home enough to enforce it. It went on for a solid hour, and I don't remember everything she said, only: *I'm ashamed to be your mother.*

A few weeks later a cop car drove slowly up our driveway and served me with papers. I was being charged with felony solicitation; one of the girls had said I told Danny to shoot. My mother asked me if that was true. I didn't remember say-ing it, although the more I thought about it, the more it seemed like I might have.

I told her I was innocent. She probably didn't believe me, but she didn't ask again.

When my court date came she put on a pantsuit I didn't know she owned, made me wear a shirt and tie, and told me on the drive to Bisbee that I'd better stand up straight and keep my smart mouth shut and at least pretend to be the boy she'd raised.

We waited in this lobby with a bunch of real delinquents, who didn't have their mothers with them, and who ignored me like the rube I was. When they called my name we went into the courtroom and my mother played the judge a tune about us moving out of state—which startled me until I real-ized it wasn't true—and couldn't he just move this case along, seeing as how it was that girl's word against her son's? She turned and pointed at me, and I stood up straight.

The judge asked the prosecution if I had any priors. Some-body said no. He looked over at me for the first and only time, sighed deeply, and said, "Son, if I dismiss these charges, will I ever see you in here again?"

I said no. He banged his gavel and that was that. Mom took me to lunch at a tourist joint on Main Street, where an old couple at the next table commented on how nice I looked in my tie, and I grinned and thanked them as Mom glared at me across the table.

Danny copped a plea, got probation and community service. I needled him for months about how I'd gotten off easy. Soon our mothers let us out of the house again, and we went back to most of our old habits, but we didn't shoot anything. That summer, Danny's mother died in her sleep. I heard he found her there in bed in the morning. When I ran into him on Allen Street the next day, he was a different person, so grown-up. I said I was sorry. He said thanks. He said he was moving to Tucson to live with his sister, and that was the last time I saw him.

A line of people stands in the courthouse lobby, waiting for passports and name changes, to get married and divorced. A rack of official forms hangs on the wall. One is the state of Arizona's *Marriage Handbook,* distributed in English or Spanish to anyone applying for a marriage license. I take one and browse the table of contents. The second half of it is about divorce.

I knew Ray was married when he met my mother, but the stack of papers I find by running his Social Security number makes the picture clearer: he and his wife of twelve years had three kids and were in bad financial straits, fifty grand in debt, their home and only vehicle in repossession. Their divorce records include his typed affidavit: *In August 1999 I separated from my family. At that time I was employed as a police officer with the City of Tombstone. I knew my tenure with them would be ending soon due to my mental and physical stability.* At the time, I hadn't known Ray was unstable—he told me he quit because of politics— and if he was, it seems like a strange thing to mention in a divorce affidavit. That's not the only mystery: at the end of his statement he says that he expects his financial situation to improve shortly, because he plans to move to another state to pursue better job opportunities. If he and my mother were planning a move, they never told me about it. I wonder if she told him to say that, trying the same trick that worked on the judge who dismissed my case.

The last paper in the stack is my mother and Ray's marriage license, which is almost as tacky as the courthouse, all baroque borders and ornate fonts. She was forty-three, on her fifth marriage; he was thirty-four, on his second. They must have been given the handbook. As I wait for copies to be made, I thumb through it. The handbook contains sections on "Addressing Economic Issues," "Taking Responsibility for Raising Children," and "Learning Effective Confrontation." I guess Ray never read it. It also has sections on "Protecting Yourself from Domestic Violence" and "Making a Personal Safety Plan." I guess Mom didn't read it either.

The first Cochise County sheriff was Johnny Behan, a political ally of the Clantons. When Behan was elected, he crawfished on a deal to make Wyatt undersheriff, and so began a long feud. Wyatt stole Behan's girlfriend, Josie, who would later become Wyatt's third wife. Behan tried to arrest the Earps after the Gunfight at the O.K. Corral, but Wyatt refused to be arrested. After the Earps left town, Behan fell out of favor in Tombstone and lost his reelection bid. To the extent that history remembers him, it's as a blowhard and a crook.

Behan's former office moved to Bisbee with the county seat. The Cochise County Sheriff's Office now occupies a complex across town from the courthouse, far from the tourist district, at the base of the Mule Mountains. The building is muted and modern, painted a myriad of tans, windows tinted, a pole outside with two flags flapping in the wind. I check in at the desk and walk straight to the bathroom, where I splash water on my face and check myself in the mirror. I'm already sweating through my shirt, and the wrinkles webbing the sleeves make me wish I'd bothered to iron it. I take a few deep breaths, walk out the door, and almost run into a man in uniform.

He greets me by name and shakes my hand. It takes me a second to realize that this is Freeney, the detective who handled my mother's case. I remember him as tall and lanky, mustached and brusque—in my memory he resembles Wyatt Earp—but instead he's shorter than me and powerfully built, handsome and clean shaven, so friendly it's a bit disarming.

As he leads me down the hall, Freeney asks about the drive to Bisbee, and cracks a joke about the photo radar unit down the street, says he hopes I wasn't speeding. He turns into a spacious office overlooking the tail end of the Mule Mountains and motions to a chair across from his enormous desk. I take my notebook out of my pocket, sit, and wonder if this was a bad idea. This big office full of plaques—Freeney's been promoted, probably several times, and it reminds me how long it's been since he handled the investigation into my mother's murder. How can I expect him to remember the details of a long-cold case when I didn't recognize him in the lobby?

A few nights before I came to see Freeney, I was lying on the guesthouse floor, sweating and drunk and alone, wondering what the hell I was doing in Arizona, following cold trails to find men who didn't remember anything worth knowing. I was sick of other people's memories. The copies of Brian's documents lay unread on the coffee table, full of facts and dates and names. I did a shot of tequila to steel myself, then sat on the floor and read it all.

The call went out from the Cochise County Sheriff's Office dispatcher at 4:26 p.m. on September 19, 2001, a warm and windy Wednesday in southeastern Arizona: the Tombstone marshal was reporting a dead body near Gleeson. The man who'd found the body—Bob, my mother's friend—had shown up at the marshal's home to report it. Gleeson was county jurisdiction, so the marshal had called it in to the sheriff. Bob said it was hard to give directions to the property, that he'd have to show someone. Sheriff's deputies Cash and Martinez responded: Cash to the marshal's house, and Martinez to the Gleeson area, where he waited for further instructions. Martinez contacted dispatch to request a medic.

Cash picked up Bob and drove east on Gleeson Road. Bob told the story of how he'd found the body. En route to the scene, they met with Martinez, who followed them to a residence located on an unmarked dirt road. The road forked and they turned west down a driveway marked with a red octagonal sign that said "WHOA," which my mother and Ray had put there as a joke. The property had one permanent structure, a shed, as well as a travel trailer, a horse corral, a horse trailer, and a boat covered by a tarp. Bob said the body was in the travel trailer. The deputies parked nearby. Cash told Bob to remain in the vehicle while the deputies assessed the scene.

The trailer's only entrance faced west. Cash and Martinez approached from the north, moving along the west wall. Cash tried the doorknob. It was unlocked. The deputies called out "Sheriff's Department" and got no response. They entered the trailer.

Inside, the deputies observed a white female lying facedown on a bed. Her feet faced north and her head faced south. She was unclothed and what appeared to be dried blood ran from her left shoulder down her arm. Her head rested on a wooden shelf or headboard, and more blood was visible on the back left side of her head, as well as a large pool of blood on the wood. The body showed signs of lividity.

An assault rifle, possibly an AK-47, was propped barrel-up against the wall on the left side of the bed. Cash walked down the hall and found a bolt-action rifle in the bathroom. Martinez noticed a crossword puzzle book near the body. He got the impression that she was reading it at the time of her death. A call came over the radio that an ambulance was on scene. After verifying that nobody else was in the residence, Cash and Martinez exited.

The ambulance couldn't make it up the driveway, so the medics walked from the gate. They were advised of the situation and told to disturb the body as little as possible. Martinez accompanied them inside the residence. The medics confirmed that lividity had set in and that there were no signs of life. They found what appeared to be two puncture wounds in the left shoulder blade and another on the left side of the woman's head. The medics contacted Tucson Medical Center for a field pronouncement. She was pronounced dead at 5:36 p.m.

While the others were inside, Cash searched the surrounding area for more victims, but found none. The medics and Martinez exited the trailer, and Martinez asked Cash to photograph the body. He reentered the trailer and took four Polaroids. The officers taped off a perimeter to establish a crime scene and radioed dispatch to report a possible homicide. Cash spoke with Commander Russell and asked him to respond to the scene. A crime scene tech was called in, as was another detective.

More Cochise County sheriff's personnel arrived over the course of the next few hours. A search warrant for the premises was requested, granted, and executed. Two detectives were assigned to search the outbuildings; another sketched and measured the trailer; others took video and 35 mm photographs; and one took digital photographs and assisted in finding evidence. Freeney arrived on the scene. He would lead the investigation from then on, including interviewing us a few days later.

He did a walk-around of the structure and saw no signs of forced entry and no indications of a struggle on the ground outside. He noted the weather conditions—clear skies and a temperature in the high fifties—and the lighting: the detectives used flashlights inside the trailer, and exterior lights powered by a generator. The scene was photographed, videotaped, diagrammed, and processed for fingerprints; meanwhile, Freeney assessed the condition of the body. He noted fly activity and deduced from blood seepage and lividity that she had been lying on her left side, facing the window, prior to death. He surveyed the trailer, which was unkempt and cluttered, and collected and logged potential evidence, including four .25 caliber shell casings, miscellaneous papers and pictures, a computer, and bottles of prescription medications. He told the tech to process the front door for prints. None were found.

Freeney called the medical examiner for permission to remove the body and received it. People from the funeral home arrived just after midnight. Upon removing the body, they discovered that the gunshot wound to the head was in fact multiple wounds. Freeney finished processing the scene and left an evidence receipt on the counter, along with a copy of the search warrant. The detectives did a final walk-through and left the scene at 1:08 a.m. on September 20.

At approximately one o'clock the following afternoon, an autopsy was performed by the Pima County medical examiner. It was learned that the deceased had been shot eight times, twice in the shoulder and six times in the head. During the autopsy, my brother, who had just learned of my mother's death from Connie, called the office and described our mother. The body was identified as Deborah St. Germain–Hudson.

I finished reading and sat staring at the empty fireplace. The ceiling fan clicked overhead and a siren sounded far away. In the morning I called Freeney to set up this meeting. He sounded surprised to hear from me after all this time, and said he wasn't sure he could tell me much about my mother's case, but he'd certainly be willing to try. He offered to give me directions, but I know this county by heart.

Freeney asks what he can do for me. I tell him I have some questions about the police report, then ask if I can record the conversation. He agrees, but I can tell by the way he looks at the recorder, his jaw setting tight, that it was a mistake.

I try to ask the first question, but begin to stammer. I'd always assumed she was shot from the front, that Ray walked in the door of the trailer and pointed the gun at her, and before he pulled the trigger, she had a brief chance for peace or terror or a dying thought. In my version of the story, she saw it coming. But when I read the police report Brian gave me, I realized that the detectives thought she'd been shot from behind. She never saw it coming. He shot her in the back.

I finally get the question out: "She was shot in the back of the shoulder? The back of the head?"

Freeney gives me a steady look, thinks for a while, and says he believes it was roughly from behind, at an angle. "Obviously, it's been a long time. I'm trying to remember."

"I have the reports." I slide the folder across his desk and he flips through the pages. For a few long minutes the room is silent except for the shuffling of paper. Above his desk hangs a motivational poster in praise of Risk. Framed certificates fill the far wall. One says he's been certified in Truth Verification. I wonder what that test is like.

The silence gets to be too much. "I don't expect you to reconstruct the whole thing. . . ."

"I'm just trying to find something." Freeney doesn't look up from the papers.

I fold my hands in my lap and wait. The window faces northwest, toward Tombstone, where dark-bottomed clouds mill in the sky, procrastinating. If a storm comes, it'll come quick, a half hour of thunderclaps and torrents. The washes in the places past those mountains, the places where we used to live, will fill with rushing water, and the desert will smell as rich as fresh blood. I wonder how many dead bodies Freeney has seen. That's what I should be asking: What does he do with them all? Does he still think of them, years later, or is there some kind of secret to forgetting?

Soon I can't help myself. "I'm just trying to figure out, because the last page of the report mentions . . . there were fingernail scrapings, under . . . matching Ray's DNA. Did it seem like there was a struggle?"

Freeney leans back in his chair and looks me in the eye. He's professional and composed, all the things I wish I were, but not unkind. "Yeah," he says. "They got into a scuffle."

"So it seemed like an escalating thing."

"Yeah. Heat of the battle," he says. "How it started, or why, I don't think we'll ever know."

"Sure," I say, but I don't believe that. By the time I'm done, I'll know.

"There was some kind of struggle," he continues. "Your mom fought back." I almost want to smile. Of course she

---

163

fought back; if he'd ever seen her alive, he wouldn't be surprised by that. His voice softens. "And at that point, the weapon was taken out."

"Right." The word comes out like a sigh. Another pause ensues. I ask about the liquor bottles. It's always bothered me: the last time we met, when he was a detective and I was a kid and I thought he was tall and thin and had a mustache, he said something about bottles. He asked if Mom and Ray drank much, and the question surprised me, because my mother drank a glass of wine a few times a year, usually at the Japanese restaurant in Sierra Vista, that sweet plum wine they served. She'd order it guiltily, saying she never drank—as if we didn't know that—but she loved that wine. I'd think of my friends' parents in the bars on Allen Street every night, my father's boilermakers in front of the TV when I went to visit, and her so apologetic about a glass of wine with dinner. The last time we met, when I said she didn't drink, Freeney had said that they found a lot of empty bottles. The police report didn't mention it. Freeney thinks for a minute, says he doesn't remember anything out of the ordinary, nothing that would indicate that alcohol played a role in her death.

I ask about the gun. The police report lists dozens of items that were taken into evidence, from the scene of her death and the scene of Ray's, and in the folder in my hands I have a formal letter requesting all of those items, along with other materials related to the investigation. But the one thing I want most isn't mentioned anywhere: the murder weapon.

"Was it ever found?"

Freeney shakes his head. "He could have ditched it anywhere." He leans back in his chair, one hand resting on his belt, near the holster. It must be a cop thing: Ray used to sit just like that.

I look at my notebook. I don't have any more questions. I

haven't learned much that I couldn't read in the report, and I don't know why I expected to. Why should he still think about a murder from so long ago, an open-and-shut case of domestic violence, when he must have seen so many others since?

I turn off the recorder and thank him for meeting me, but we both stay in our chairs. I thank him for his work on my mother's case. He says he was just doing his job. I put my hands on the arms of the chair and begin to rise.

But Freeney keeps talking. He says he knew of Ray before the murder—he never met him, but law enforcement is a small world—and that all the signs of the investigation led him to believe that Ray didn't plan it. When emotions get involved, he says, you just can't account for what happens. He looks out the window. "And living in a place like that, away from society, out there in the desert . . . these things just don't conform to logic."

I know what he's offering me. The recorder's off; this is the unofficial version, his version, from a man who's seen enough to know how these things work. He knows that you can seek the truth, dig up documents and artifacts, interview witnesses, examine the evidence, and use that information to construct a narrative that serves a purpose: this is how it happened. An official story. The truth. But it never really adds up; it never makes sense. *These things just don't conform to logic.*

He's also warning me. If I keep pursuing this, expecting to find an answer, expecting the who and when and how to lead me to a why, it'll never end. There is no why. *Why* is such an asshole of a word.

I could stop now, put this behind me, try to move on. Do I really need to see what I'm about to ask for: the rest of the report, the things they took from that trailer, the jewelry they took off of her body? A thousand miles from here, I've built a different life. I don't need to be circling this place, sifting through the past. Freeney has a point, and I know he means well. He seems like a kind and decent man, although it's not that hard to seem like any kind of man. But Freeney doesn't understand, because that body he found out in the desert years ago wasn't his mother.

I hand him the letter. He reads it, says he'll send me whatever he can find, but most of it has probably been destroyed by now. We exchange business cards and he walks me out. At the door he shakes my hand and says goodbye. On my way across the parking lot, I look out past the jail at the cloud shadows on the mountains. *A place like that, away from society, out there in the desert.*

But how far is it to a place like that? High Lonesome Road is about a mile east of here, and it leads straight north to Gleeson. She died just on the other side of those mountains, two turns and twenty miles from Freeney's office.

As I leave the sheriff's complex, I see a small plane circling in the sky to the east, above the community college airport where my mother did her pilot training. Once, on a solo flight, she flew into a summer storm like the one brewing right now. The clouds blew in from nowhere, and she found herself blind inside them, panicked, longing to see the ground, some kind of landmark. But she couldn't find anything, and soon she couldn't tell which way was down. It was as if the sky had swallowed her. It occurred to her that she might die.

She thought of her sons. We were almost grown, and there were worse ways to go—it was peaceful there in the cloud, and at least she was on an adventure, doing something she loved. But she wanted to send a message to us, as she always had before she jumped out of planes, in case she didn't make it.

She didn't have a pen or paper, and knew a note would burn in the crash. So she closed her eyes and concentrated, sent us a message through the air: *Boys, be strong. I love you.* Then she prayed.

The sky opened the moment she said Amen. She was out of the cloud; she was safe. After she landed, driving home, she kept thinking of that moment in the cloud, the sense of peace. Later that night, when she told me the story, she asked if I'd heard her message. I told her the truth: I hadn't heard anything.

UNCLE TOM'S HOUSE

Days pass, hot and stormy, as I wait for Freeney's package. I talk to Laura on the phone, read books I've already read, sit on the stoop watching trash blow by in the empty street. When I can stomach it, I dig through the box of my mother's things. I find some photos that my mother must have taken of Uncle Tom and his kids. After Max, before Ray, my mother had custody of her brother's children for about a year. Tom was in trouble again, unemployed and bingeing, and the state took his kids away. My mother brought them to live with us. I was still grounded from the pellet-gun incident, so she made me babysit when she was at work.

Tom came to visit on the weekends. He and my mother would take the kids out to the horse corrals. The boys, Sean and Eric, were only four and five, scared of horses, and they held their father's hand and hid behind his legs and watched the animals with faces full of awe. I think Tom was scared of the horses, too, but he didn't show it to his kids. He would tell the boys funny lies, that horses were dinosaurs, that he could speak their language. Leighanne, the oldest, just a few years older than her brothers but more like a mother to them, smiled and played along, although she knew all about horses by then, things my mother had taught her, how to feed them halved apples from her flattened palm, to keep a hand on their rumps when you walked behind them and stay close to their hind legs so they wouldn't kick.

My mother loved to watch her brother with his kids. It was the only time I ever saw her recede like that, making herself scarce, becoming an observer. She would disappear into the barn, where it was cool and dark and sweet with the smells of alfalfa and leather, and she would stay there until I began to worry about snakes. Every few months we'd catch one hiding in the pallets, and she almost got bit once, not paying attention, arms full of hay, hearing the rattle too late and coming face-to-face with it, coiled between the slats, tail shaking so fast it was invisible, more of a hum than a rattle. She handled it well, didn't panic, backed slowly away until she was out of reach. Then she grabbed a rake, pinned its head to the ground, and cut it off with a shovel.

She'd come out of the barn, holding flakes of hay, and she'd hand them to Tom so he could fling them to the horses and let his children see him taking care of something. He was clean at the time. We all hoped it would stick.

A man behind a bulletproof window takes my ID and directs me to the Tucson Police Department records office, where a woman behind another window stares at me and says nothing. I tell her I'm looking for a police report. She asks a few basic questions, but I don't know the answers, only that a body was found and the approximate date.

"Do you know who it was?"

"My uncle."

Her face retains its bored expression; she's used to this, has seen it all. I'm starting to prefer this response. "Was he killed?"

"I don't think so."

She hands me a form. I sit and fill it out, then hand it back to her. She glances at it and asks if I know where he was found.

"An abandoned building. I don't know what part of town." My brother called me after it happened, told me the story secondhand, said only that it was somewhere in Tucson.

She says she'll see what she can find, and returns a few minutes later, dangling a document from two pinched fingers. She charges me fifty cents and slides the paper through the gap in the window, looking directly into my eyes and holding it for a long, unnerving second before she tells me to have a nice day. I wait until I'm outside, in my car in the parking lot with the air-conditioning blasting, to read the report.

In October of 2005, the caretaker of an abandoned house in central Tucson went by to check on the property and noticed that a window had been forced open. He called the police. The responding officer entered the building and found a dead man lying on a mattress next to syringes and a spoon. On a nearby shelf were a prison release card and papers bearing my uncle's name. The officer took pictures, collected evidence, called the medical examiner, and left. That's it; that's the end of the report. The police report of my mother's death is more than fifty pages. Uncle Tom got two.

When I'm done, I toss the papers onto the passenger seat and stare at a crumbling stucco wall. My mother used to worry that I'd end up like Tom; instead they ended up the same, both found dead in a deserted place.

When I lived in Tombstone, signs along the boardwalk marked where people had been killed. Outside the Oriental, where Wyatt once ran the faro game, was a sign saying that Marshal White had been shot dead in that spot by Curly Bill Brocious, in what was later ruled an accident. At the former site of Campbell and Hatch's pool hall stood a sign commemorating Morgan Earp's death. I liked the signs, thought they were a fitting gesture to the victims.

The house in Tucson where my uncle died has a For Sale sign out front. The derelict building described in the report is gone, demolished and replaced by a freshly painted duplex. The gravel driveway is smooth and pristine, with no tire tracks or footprints, and a new plank fence surrounds the yard. The building looks brand-new, like nothing ever happened here. For a moment I think about calling the number on the sign and asking how much it costs. I could buy it and burn it down.

When Tom was squatting in the house that used to be here, fresh out of prison, cooking up his last hit, I was living a few miles away. I hadn't seen or heard from him since he squeezed my shoulder and then vanished at my mother's funeral mass, but I knew he was somewhere nearby. I wonder why he never tried to call me, if he was ashamed, if he thought I was. He might have assumed that I wouldn't want to see my junkie uncle, to be reminded of a former life. If so, he was probably right. I was in grad school when he died, had just spent the summer in Europe, had my own apartment and all kinds of theories, one of which was that I deserved that better life because I'd lost someone. Tom lost someone, too, his sister, his rock. He got a bag of heroin, a box of needles, and a mattress in a stranger's house to die on. Nobody deserves what they get.

CHANCE

———

My old college friend Orion calls, says he heard I was in Tucson, and invites me to a barbecue at his house. He's turning thirty. At his party, I see a lot of Orion's former coworkers from the French Quarter, some of the same faces I saw the night we heard about my mother. They looked much younger then.

I find Orion and his family by the pool and we start to catch up. I ask if Chance is here.

"He's hiding," Orion says.

"From what?"

He shrugs and gestures indiscriminately, at the sky, at the swimmers in the pool. "He hides from everything."

I find Chance in the corner of the bathroom, his head shoved deep into the space between the toilet and the tub. I call his name and he doesn't move. I sit on the edge of the tub and pet him, rub behind his ears how he used to like, and still he doesn't move.

———

In the movie *Tombstone,* during the scene in which Morgan Earp is dying, his dog paces the doorway of the pool hall, barking up a storm. Finally, Wyatt yells for somebody to get rid of the goddamned dog. That really happened: according to a newspaper account, after Morgan died, the dog even followed his master's body as it was carried to the undertaker. I wonder what happened to that dog afterward, whether Wyatt adopted it, if it became a stray.

Chance lived with me for about a year after the murder. He seemed to know what had happened: he was afraid of loud noises, hated to be left alone. During thunderstorms he'd cower in the bathroom, nose stuck in a corner, whimpering. One day I left him inside while I went to the grocery store across the street and he jumped through a plate-glass window and greeted me at the gate, trailing blood from gashes in his snout.

I asked the vet if she saw this kind of thing a lot.

"If there's some kind of trauma, sure. Abuse, abandonment. Sometimes moving into a new house will do it." She told me I should try a counselor and gave me a business card for the Dog Whisperer.

"You're kidding."

"Sometimes it works," she said. "You'd be surprised."

I didn't call the Dog Whisperer. I'd just tried a shrink myself, a counselor on campus, who'd said I was coping well, and that when I felt sad I should think of a safe and peaceful place. When I tried it, I saw a beach. I don't like beaches, but my mother did.

Chance got worse. I tried leaving him in my bedroom and he ate through a doorjamb. I bought him a crate and he broke it, ate through an ocotillo fence and ran away. At the pound he huddled in the corner of his cage, watching silently as the doomed dogs around him whined and howled. My landlord saw the damage he'd done and threatened to evict me. Orion had a dog that was friends with Chance, and being around other dogs was the only thing that calmed him down. Orion said he'd take him temporarily. That was seven years ago.

Orion appears in the doorway of the bathroom. Chance still hasn't moved.

"Is he always like this?"

"Pretty much. He's on drugs." Orion opens the medicine cabinet and tosses me an orange prescription bottle. "They're for humans, but the vet said they'd work."

The pills don't seem to be doing Chance much good. I have to pry him out of the corner, and only then do I see how old he looks, his whiskers gone white, slow in his motions, so thin in the haunches that it makes me cringe. I lead him into the hall, pet him, talk to him, but there's no response, no recognition in those wet black eyes, no wolfish smile like the one he used to give.

"At least he hasn't bit me."

"He can't," Orion says. "His teeth are gone." He says a few weeks ago he left Chance at home during a thunderstorm, and he bit through his crate and jumped out a picture window. Orion found him at the pound. The vet pulled his broken teeth. Orion got a thicker window. Chance got pills.

Orion returns to the party. Chance shoves his snout into my shin. I sit on the floor and hold his head in my hands and knead the thick fur around his neck. His eyes have been dulled by age and medication, but they still look sad and scared. I whisper his name. He doesn't lick my hand, doesn't whine like he used to. On the drive over here I imagined taking him home with me, but that was a fantasy. I'm not sure he remembers me, and even if he does, he must know I'm going to walk out that door again and leave him behind. We have different lives now, in different places, where nobody knows or cares about our pasts. We're both better off this way.

But he's still afraid of thunder.

My hands dig into his fur. He looks away, then back at me.

Chance.

Tell me what you saw.

GUN

———

A lot of factors caused the Gunfight at the O.K. Corral—rivalries and rumormongering, broken deals and betrayals, business and political tensions—but in the most literal sense it was a fight over gun control. The usual boomtown violence, and especially Curly Bill's killing of Marshal White, prompted the citizens of Tombstone to pass an ordinance banning firearms within the city limits. The day of the gunfight, Virgil Earp was repeatedly told that the Clantons were at the O.K. Corral, carrying weapons. He would later claim that he only went down there to disarm them.

San Francisco passed a similar law in 2005, banning handguns in the city limits, but it was ruled unconstitutional. I first tried to buy the gun that killed my mother there, at the last gun store left in the city, only to be told that the model wasn't approved for sale in California. When I first got to Tucson, I tried every gun store in town with no luck. One owner told me the distributor was sold out because there had been a run on handguns and ammo since Obama's election. He told me to try the gun show.

I get there around noon, and it's a hundred in the shade, the parking lot bleached and wavy in the sun. Near the entrance a bunch of sweaty white people in straw hats wave clipboards and shout idiotic slogans about socialism, trying to get me to sign some petition. I don't acknowledge them, and neither do the other people walking past. We're not here to talk politics, we just want air-conditioning.

I've never been to a gun show before, and the scene in the lobby is not what I expected. The staff is young and respectable, smiling and polite. They wear shirts with sleeves. A teenage blonde behind the counter checks Facebook as I buy a ticket for eight bucks. Just when I think I was wrong to expect a bunch of militia wingnuts, a man walks by wearing a sign around his neck that says, "Ask Me About Nazi Daggers."

The showroom reminds me of a small-town high school gym. Throngs of people mill around folding tables fondling guns, and private sellers carry rifles slung over their shoulders. Signs advertise the arcane alphanumerics of gun culture: AK-47, AR-15, M1911A1. A table by the entrance bears stacks of flyers, some of which make sense—the NRA, the Libertarian Party, superchurches, veterans' groups—and some of which surprise me: the Arizona Medical Marijuana Project and an upcoming science fiction and fantasy convention called FiestaCon.

Just inside the door, a young black guy waves me over to his stall. He asks what guns I own. I tell him I have a hunting rifle and a 12-gauge shotgun. He asks what I use as a lubricant, and I finally notice the banner above his head: "Gun Juice!"

"Oil," I say. "Gun oil."

"Feel this," he says, holding out the receiver of a Glock 19 and pointing at the slide. I rub my finger along the metal. It's slick. "Now rub your fingers together. What do you feel?"

"Nothing."

"Exactly. No greasy residue." He hands me the gun. "Now smell it."

"What?"

He nods. "Go on."

It must be a joke, something the sellers do to pass the time— let's see how many morons smell the gun. But nobody's watching, so I smell it.

"And what do you smell?"

"Nothing."

"See? Odorless and permanent. You'll never need another lubricant."

I walk away while he's still talking. I'm not here to buy Gun Juice; I'm here to buy a gun.

The manufacturer's website describes the Beretta 21 Bobcat as "trustworthy and precise," says it measures 4.9 inches and weighs 11.5 ounces, and comes in either .22LR or .25ACP. The .25 caliber model, which my mother had, holds eight bullets. She kept it in a nylon holster, which she carried in her saddlebag when she was riding horses, in the backseat pocket of her truck when she wasn't. It wasn't legal at the time in Arizona to carry a concealed weapon without a permit, but my mother didn't care. The laws have since been changed; now you can take one into a bar.

It was the last of many guns she owned. She qualified as expert with the M-16 in the army, and she owned a few different pistols after she got out. Most of the men she dated were former military or police, so they all had guns, too, and they'd take me shooting as a way of trying to bond with me or bribe me. The first time I shot a gun, I was six years old, and my mother was standing behind me.

And even though a gun killed her, I still own a couple. I don't love guns, don't belong to any organizations, don't have any bumper stickers. I know about the studies and statistics, all the arguments against them, and I've seen firsthand what they can do. But I sleep with a loaded shotgun under my bed for one simple reason: in case there's a man at the door who means me harm. My friends in San Francisco tell me that if that happens, I should call the police; I tell them that the police won't show up in time to save them, and will only catch their killer half the time. Nobody ever wins the argument. They don't believe in the man at the door. I do. I've met him.

At the far end of the room, stalls sell everything but guns. The T-shirt section is a pageant of insanity: one has a picture of President Obama next to Hitler and Saddam Hussein, and another features a Browning sniper rifle, which in expert hands can kill a person from a mile away, above the slogan "When in Doubt, Vote from the Rooftops." A book table displays a manual for building a fallout shelter, a state-by-state guide to gun laws, and a doorstop of a novel that claims to double as a survivalist handbook. Knives are everywhere, pocket knives and boot knives and tactical knives, sais and samurai swords and steak knife sets, streams of glinting steel. Signs advertise everything from glitter paint to hand lotion to jerky made from the meat of a dozen different animals. Half the stalls here hang at least one flag, and a few sell nothing but them: current and historical versions of the American flag in every conceivable size, as well as the usual gun-culture suspects: the Confederate battle flag, the black POW/MIA flag, the yellow

"Don't Tread on Me" flag, and the flags of various ancestral European nations.

As I observe the crowd, I can't help but think that based on sheer statistics, there are a half-dozen convicted murderers in this room. A few booths down, a group of young men with prison tats on their muscular arms cradle assault-rifle components. They pay for their purchases with thick wads of cash. In a few days, the *Arizona Daily Star*'s cover story will be about drug cartels buying weapons at gun shows. Still, the majority of the gun-show people prove to be friendly and helpful. It takes a little while to get used to the guns everywhere, all of which seem to be pointing at me, and the crowd is overwhelmingly white and male and Republican, but otherwise the atmosphere reminds me of any other hobbyist gathering, antique shows or chili cook-offs or comic book conventions. A man with a baby on his back and two rifles in his arms walks past me, and as I move out of his way, I see it, lying amid a spread of semiautomatics: a Beretta Model 21 in .25ACP. The gun I came here for.

I pick it up. The entire pistol fits in my palm. It looks like a toy. I expected to feel something, holding it again, but I don't feel much. It's just a piece of metal, a light cool weight in my hand.

I first saw the gun that killed my mother on Christmas. One of the videotapes in the camera bag I took from my brother's house is a home movie of that morning. It begins with Ray behind the camera, filming Josh and me as we mock the scraggly tree Mom bought at Walmart. For the first few minutes, the camera avoids my mother; she's a voice offscreen. Finally, once we've begun to open presents, it pans to her, in a red

Western shirt and jeans, her brown hair cut into bangs, the hairstyle she'd settled on decades before and stuck with. Seeing her reminds me again how poorly I remember who she really was, what she looked like, how she spoke, all the parts of her I've already lost.

She sits on the floor; Josh and I are on the couch, but neither of us offers to move. As she opens a package of body spray, Ray speaks from behind the camera, continuing a debate we'd been having about the definition of the word *eve*. He thinks Christmas Eve is a misnomer, that Christmas Eve should mean tonight, the night of Christmas. Earlier, I consulted the dictionary and proved him wrong, but he won't let it go.

"So what do you call tonight, then?" he asks.

Josh and Mom and I exchange looks. "Christmas Night," I say, with a little too much satisfaction.

Mom says she doesn't want to open any more of her presents, that she wants us to open ours. Josh opens the socks I bought him and we argue over whether they're blue or black. Mom wonders if he's color-blind. That's how it always was with her: if we were thirsty, we had diabetes.

She takes the camera, and Ray fills the frame. He's smiling and eager as he opens his present. It's his first Christmas with us. I got them matching sweatshirts. He makes a big show of how much he likes his, holds it up to his chest, talks about how warm it must be. This was just when we were starting to get along.

Josh and I are next. We unwrap our biggest presents and discover that Mom has bought us each our first computers. We're awed by the gesture, because computers were still expensive then, and she didn't have that kind of money. She was working at the Mexican restaurant at the time, and Ray didn't have a job at all. Those computers meant a lot of long nights feeding tourists, a lot of other things she couldn't buy for herself. In retrospect, it shouldn't have surprised us: it was another in a long line of sacrifices.

The camera turns to me, a close-up shot. I'm wearing a white T-shirt and baggy jeans, and my hair is long and ridiculous, almost a mullet. A silver crucifix hangs around my neck. My mother gave me that; when she died, I stopped wearing it. I stare at myself on the screen, ten years younger, and wish I could warn him.

This younger version of me asks the camera where Tom is. He was living with us at the time—I hadn't ratted him out yet for shooting up in the bathroom. The camera turns away, and my mother's voice drops. "Sleeping. He'll be out soon." The time stamp in the bottom corner says it was filmed at one in the afternoon. Tom never appears in the video.

Ray opens another gift, from Connie and Bob. It's a circular metal sign with two unicorns on it touching horns. He reads the tag and says it symbolizes peace and contentment, that it's a blessing, like having a cross somewhere. It was hanging in the corral when he killed her. My mother opens the next present, from me, a portable stereo she said she wanted for the horse trailer. I saw it that day we went in the trailer, spattered with blood.

The presents continue, more clothes, wallets, watches, the toothbrushes and dumb gag gifts she put in our stockings. My brother tries on a belt and we argue over whether it's too small. He was heavy then; he's slimmed down since. It's been so long.

The tape ends abruptly right before she opened her last gift. A small package, she held it in one hand and peeled the paper back with the other. The room went quiet for a moment when she realized what it was, as she took the gun from the box and turned it over in her hands, treating it with the peculiar awe we afford instruments of death. She stood and hugged my brother, mumbling into his shoulder that he shouldn't have spent so much money on her. She had tears in her eyes. I remember looking at that stupid stereo and wishing I had thought to buy her a gun instead.

We passed the Beretta around as Josh told the story of how he'd bought it. He saw it for sale in the newspaper classifieds, called the number in the ad, and spoke to an old lady who said her son had bought it for her and she didn't want it. Josh went to her house, gave her cash, and left with the gun. All of which was and is perfectly legal, in Arizona and in most other states.

The Beretta 21 I'm holding is the only one I've seen here. The tag says three hundred and nineteen dollars. When the guy behind the table asks if he can help me, I tell him I'll take it.

He leads me around to the far side of the table, carrying the gun, and hands me a clipboard full of forms. The first is U.S. Bureau of Alcohol, Tobacco, and Firearms Form 4473, the document that records most firearm transactions in America. It asks for the same information as any government form: my full name and address, place and date of birth, height and weight, gender, Social Security number (which is optional), race (which isn't), and citizenship. Below those boxes is a list of yes or no questions: *Are you the actual buyer of the firearm listed on this form? Are you a fugitive from justice? Have you been convicted in any court of a misdemeanor crime of domestic violence?*

As I complete the form, he makes small talk with a woman standing nearby, browsing the handguns. "Have you seen our pink guns?" he asks.

"I'm all set, thanks." She smiles tightly and wanders away.

I hand him the form and he asks for my ID. I show him my California license.

He snatches the gun off the table. "Sorry," he says. "Can't

sell to you." The genial gun seller has disappeared, replaced by a cool cop-like suspicion.

"Why not?"

"Against the law. Sorry." He turns abruptly and walks away.

I ask around and learn that because I live in another state, I can't buy a gun from a dealer here. At this gun show, I can buy Nazi daggers, a samurai sword, throwing stars, lavender hand lotion, alligator jerky, and Gun Juice, but I can't buy a gun.

Late one night just before I moved away from home, half asleep, I heard a sound outside, a car engine roaring, coming closer. Ray met me in the hallway, said he had heard it, too. Together we walked in silence through the dark trailer. On the landing we stood watching. Headlights cast a halo above a hill to the east. The noise of the engine had quieted but we could still hear the faint thrum of its idle.

Ray asked me in a whisper about my rifle. I told him it was under my bed.

"Go get it."

I hesitated. The car was probably kids, teenagers heading to a party in the boonies, maybe even some of my friends. At worst it might be a coyote driving a load of illegals, but they wouldn't pose a threat to us. There was no good reason to get the gun.

But I did. By the time I returned with the rifle, the strange vehicle, a white van, had crested the hill and stopped in a flat stretch of road on the far side of the neighbor's horse corrals. Ray took the rifle from me, grabbed a flashlight from the kitchen drawer, and started walking. I tried to follow, but there wasn't much of a moon to see by, and I couldn't keep up in the dark without a light of my own. We came to a gate that led through the fence onto the neighbor's property. Ray hurried through. I stayed behind. When I turned back to our trailer, I saw the curtains in my mother's bedroom window part. I couldn't see her, but she was watching. I wonder if she had her gun, too, if she stood at the window clutching that little Beretta, if it made her feel safe.

And I wonder what she felt as she watched Ray's shadow bobbing in the flashlight beam, as he reached the road and raised the rifle to his shoulder, approaching the van and yelling something we couldn't hear, gesturing violently with the barrel, as the van slowly backed away, and as Ray returned, breathing hard, speaking fast, excited, saying it was a group of illegals and he'd told the driver to turn around or else he'd shoot. Did she think what I said afterward, that what he'd done was reckless and absurd? Who did he think he was, Wyatt Earp? Or did she feel what I secretly had while watching him, that terrible admiration, the wish that I were capable of doing something like that? Was she afraid of Ray then, or was he still her hero?

SCRAPBOOKING

A few days after the gun show and less than a mile from where it was held, I go to a meeting in a rundown hospital complex. I park in a vast and nearly empty lot and walk through the automatic doors before I have time to reconsider. Past the waiting room and down a bright echoing hall three young nurses sit behind a counter talking. They stop when they see me. One smiles and leans over the counter, asking if she can help.

"Can you tell me where Conference Room B is?"

"No." She's cute: bangs, blue scrubs, the whole nurse thing. In other circumstances I'd flirt back.

"I'm here for the Parents of Murdered Children meeting."

"Oh." She straightens and points down a hallway. "Turn left, all the way at the end."

The hallway stretches forever, waxed linoleum and fluorescent lights and posters reminding me of potential dangers. At the far end a metal door is propped open. I duck into a men's room, splash water on my face, fight down the urge to leave.

I first heard of Parents of Murdered Children a long time ago, when somebody mentioned it after my mother's death and said it was for anyone who'd lost a relative to murder, not just parents. I found and read an article about the organization that explained the typical effects of a loved one's murder: numbness, guilt, rage, insomnia, paranoia, hopelessness, depression, loss of faith, and an obsession with reconstructing the events. But I never actually came to a meeting until now, after weeks stuck in a sweltering guesthouse sifting through my mother's things, reading descriptions of her murder scene, listening to the voices of my former fathers on my tape recorder. I need to see if I'm really as alone as I feel, or if there are others.

Walking in that door will mean surrendering my scorn for the kind of people who go to meetings and talk to strangers about their problems. And I'll be violating the code of the American man, to project strength, suffer in silence, all that macho bullshit. But where has that gotten me?

The conference room is warm and slightly musty, and although it's on the first floor, it feels subterranean, like somebody's basement. A handful of people sit scattered around folding tables arranged in a rough square. A thickset white guy in his fifties sees me first. He asks what I'm looking for, and I tell him I'm here for the POMC meeting.

He sinks a little in his chair. "Yeah. This is it."

I take a seat at the far end of his table and look around. A woman about his age sits next to him, probably his wife, and next to her is a younger woman wearing the uniform of a pest control company, who seems to be their daughter. Two white ladies at another table talk loudly about traffic. Across the way, a teenage girl plays with her cell phone; the flowers tattooed on her forearms twitch as she texts. At the table by the window, a middle-aged woman with a motherly bearing, sensible clothes and makeup and hair, shuffles papers. I run the numbers: nine people, not including me; seven women, two men; five are white, three Latino, one black. Their ages run from twenty to sixty-five or so. Judging solely by appearance, especially clothes and shoes, the one constant here is that everyone is working-class, which makes sense, because so are a disproportionate number of the murder victims in America. The survivors fidget, look tired and bloodless in this bad light, make eye contact and hold it for uncomfortable amounts of time. Their pain is obvious and unguarded; if I saw these people in the supermarket, I'd know they'd lost someone. They're greenhorns: they haven't learned to hide it yet.

"Has your case gone to trial?"

The mother at my table is staring at me, waiting for an answer. This is how you make small talk here.

"No. He killed himself."

"Oh. We're still waiting for the trial." Her face is pretty, or once was—high cheekbones and smooth skin and long eyelashes—but whatever medication she's taking for the grief makes her eyes dull and vacant, her voice slow and disconcertingly calm. I still haven't seen her blink.

"I hope he fries."

"Thanks."

I assumed the killer was male, and later, when we tell our stories, I'll learn that I was right: everyone in this room lost their loved one to an angry man.

The meeting is supposed to start at 8:00. At 8:05 I'm planning my escape. I ask the pest control lady if there's a soda machine around. She says she doesn't know. I say I'll take a look and rise to leave, figuring I'm home free, until the father pipes up and says there's a soda machine at the far end of the building.

"I'll show you," he says. "C'mon."

As he leads me through the labyrinth of the hospital, he says he works in facilities maintenance for the HMO that runs this place. I tell him that's what my father does. He says he doesn't do it anymore, actually—he got laid off last month. "Forced retirement," he says, shaking his head. "Worked here for thirty years. They said it was the economy." He pauses. His face is florid, his upper lip curled. He's seething; of course he feels it too, that all-consuming rage. "The economy," he says again.

He shows me the soda machine. I buy a Coke. On the way back to the meeting, we talk about real estate prices and the Cardinals' chances of making it to the Super Bowl again, anything other than the fact that in the last year he's lost his job and his son, both for reasons he can't understand.

Back in Conference Room B, the chapter leader—the sensible housewife, whose name is Kate—explains today's activity. We're scrapbooking. She's brought boxes and bins and bags full of supplies, stickers and scissors and glue, construction paper in every conceivable color. She spreads the supplies on a table and tells us to take what we want. We were supposed to bring pictures of our loved ones; she mentioned that at the last meeting. Everyone but me is holding a picture of a victim, and I realize for the first time that they all know one another. They come here every month. I'm the outsider, the new guy, and I didn't bring any pictures.

Kate sees me still standing by the door.

"If you don't have a picture, that's OK," she says, smiling gently and waving toward my seat. "You can make the page and bring it next time."

Few things make me as uncomfortable as organized classroom activities, arts and crafts, skits, that sort of thing, and apparently I'm not the only one. The sedated woman mutters that she doesn't think she wants to do this, but sifts through the box in front of her anyway and picks a pink background. The others begin to leaf through paper scraps and make desultory attempts to settle on a color palette. Kate tells us that the pages we make will go into a big scrapbook at headquarters, a scrapbook that only other survivors will see. I try to imagine it, a white three-ring binder sitting in a storeroom in some strip mall in Mesa, the book of Arizona murder victims. I'm not putting my mother in that book.

But I can't just leave. I can make it through one meeting. So I sit and pick a few pieces of paper in earth tones, brown and green and tan, thinking I'll do something subtle. Kate comes over to my table carrying a bag of stickers.

"Who was your loved one?"

"My mother."

She leans over my shoulder and touches the pieces of paper on the table in front of me, arranging them into a pattern. She shows me where the pictures could go, and points to a spot above them. "You could put her name here, or 'Mom.'"

I grab a sheet of letters from the bag.

"And then you can put other things on the sides here, give it some color." She dumps the bag on the table, spreads the packages of stickers and looks through them. It's a lot of stickers. I ask her if she bought them all herself, and she quietly says yes, but not to worry about it, she has more than she needs. "What did she like?" she asks.

The question takes me by surprise, forces me to think about my mother as a person, as something other than the reason for my grief. Maybe scrapbooking serves a purpose after all. What *did* she like?

"Horses. She liked horses."

"That's a good start. I've got horses in here somewhere. What else?"

I take a slow and deliberate breath. She means well. She wants to help me remember my mother in a positive way, as a person who liked things. I don't know why that pisses me off, if it's because I can't even think of another thing she liked, or if it's because naming a couple of things a dead person liked is an easy way to seal them off from the complex world of the living, for whom likes and dislikes can still change. She liked horses and men, but that's not who she was.

"She really liked horses." I spot a sheet of horse-head stickers in the heap and pluck it out. Satisfied, Kate moves on to the next person.

The other night I took one of the unmarked tapes from my mother's camera bag, put it in the VCR, and saw her with her horses. It begins as she's feeding one from a bucket. Behind her looms the peak of Sheep's Head Mountain. The date in the bottom left corner is December 28, 1999. That was before she and Ray set out on their Adventure, when they were still testing out the idea by spending two weeks at a time camping and riding horses in remote parts of Arizona.

Ray filmed it. At first, she doesn't know she's on camera. A black baseball cap casts shade across her face. She looks younger than I remember her, but that might be because the tape is old, the image grainy. As the horse feeds, she leans forward and whispers in its ear, but her words are inaudible. She turns and sees the camera, and a smile breaks across her face. I pressed rewind and watched the smile spread again.

Hi, everybody!

She introduces the horse, Crook, and kisses it between its

eyes. Ray hands her the camera and she films him as he gives a tour of their campground. Mom was no auteur: the picture is shaky and zooms in and out randomly. Chance darts around the bottom of the frame as Ray leads the camera through their tent, a three-room nylon dome in peach and blue and green that casts colored spots onto his face and makes him look, in his jeans and boots and undershirt, like a rodeo clown. He carries a flashlight in one pocket and a pair of gloves in the other, and a key ring and a Leatherman dangle from his belt. He's not wearing a gun.

Mom talks to the camera as if it were her mother. This tape was intended for Grandma, to show her what her daughter's life was like. My mother points to objects and identifies them in a shrill lilt; she did that often, affecting a girlish tone, and I never understood why, if she thought it was endearing, if she thought it was expected. She must have meant her voice to sound peppy, but instead it just sounds strained, and her observations are bizarrely literal. *This is the horse's butt. There are the mountains. Here is our truck.* She films the propane stove they cook on, the campfire where they burn their trash, the bucket they use as a toilet.

I thought I'd be riveted by the tape, and for the first few minutes I was: seeing her face, hearing her voice again. But soon I couldn't avoid the thought: this is boring. I fast-forwarded, looking for clues, finding none. Did she really think Grandma would care about the spice rack? Who gives a shit about their coolers? Didn't she understand that nobody else was fascinated by her harebrained horse-trailer lifestyle?

Hi, everybody! Who's everybody? Who did she expect to see this? She had almost two years left to live, but never sent the tape to Grandma. It sat in its bag for years. I'm probably the only person who's ever watched it; I'm the only one who wants to remember. And even though I knew better, watching

---

192

it made me wonder if it was really made for me, if somehow she knew I would need it.

I'm arranging stickers around phantom photos of my mother when the girl with the tattoos sits at my table and starts to sift through the supplies. She looks over at my page and gets up. A minute later she returns and slides two pictures across the table. One is a teenage girl with her boyfriend. The other is the same girl petting a black lab.

"Here, use mine." She gives a little smile. "Until you have your own."

I look at the pictures again. Her sister, I guess. Somebody killed this girl. I thank her and ask about her sister. She tells me the story, bluntly and briefly. Like most of the stories I'll hear today, it's worse than mine. For her, it's only been six months, and most of the rest lost their loved ones in the last year. They have a name for it: the zombie phase. Like any group of experts, these people have an entire jargon all their own, acronyms and legal terminology, cities where retreats and conferences are held—*Kate's going to Kansas City this year,* someone says—police officials they refer to by their first names. They don't discuss the phases after the zombie phase: the denial phase, the rage phase, the writing-a-book-about-it phase.

Pictures of a murdered stranger rest on my mother's scrapbook page. The meeting isn't over for another hour, so I start decorating. First, her name goes in the top corner, just Debbie, because nobody ever called her Deborah, and she had too many last names to choose from—there aren't enough letters in the sheet. Beneath her name I put her dates of birth and death. A string of horses down the right side of the page as an accent, a few gold-foil leaves in one corner. Near the bottom of the sticker bag I find a quote from Thoreau: *There is no remedy for love but to love more.* She probably never read him; I never finished *Walden* myself. But the sentiment seems fitting for my mother, so I test it out in a few different locations, and settle on an open space across the bottom. By the time Kate tells us to take a break, my fingers are sticky with purple glue and the page in front of me looks like a lunatic's bumper.

I look around at the others. Most of them are done, and a few are working through the break to finish. We're naturals. It makes sense. We all do this every day: focus on a series of small and meaningless tasks to pass the time, try to preserve our memories without wallowing in grief, and hope our lives will add up to some kind of tribute. Of course we're good at scrapbooking. Scraps are all we have.

Kate comes around collecting our pages. She stops next to me and puts her hand on my shoulder. "It's nice," she says. "She would have liked it."

I suppress a flash of anger as she walks away. This happens a lot when women old enough to be my mother hear that I lost mine: they dote on me. Sometimes it's nice, but mostly it reminds me that if my real mother were still alive, I'd still be squirming out of hugs and wiping kisses off my cheek.

A clipboard stacked with petitions makes its way around. When it gets to me, I start to read the first page—something about denying parole to a murderer—before realizing that I'm not going to sit in this room, with these people, and debate whether the punishments are fitting, whether they really do anything to address the violence. I sign them all.

The break ends. Kate says it's time to introduce ourselves. "Most of us know each other's stories," she says, taking care not to look at me, "but we have new people today."

And so, before most of them even know my name, they tell me how their loved ones died. The only rule of POMC meetings is that what's said in the room stays there, but I don't need to tell their stories. Watch the news. So many people are murdered in America with such inconceivable frequency that the stories and statistics have lost their impact. Every victim has parents, spouses, siblings, kids. If all the relatives of murder victims in Arizona showed up to this meeting, this room wouldn't be big enough. This hospital wouldn't be big enough.

But the rest are somewhere else tonight. Only ten of us are here. And what I'll remember from their stories, even more than the sheer arbitrary horror of the events, is the rage they feel. They dream aloud of retribution, ghastly forms of torture. Like all rage, theirs dehumanizes: their faces twist, their eyes flare like a villain's, crazed voices come out of their mouths. I recognize their rage, share it, and know why it exists. They want impossible things, justice and revenge, resurrections and reunions, their old lives back. But all they get is pity, even from me, and soon I'll probably forget their stories, like the rest of the world already has.

My turn comes. I don't know what to say. I've been listening so intently that I haven't rehearsed.

"I'm Justin. This is my first time here." They welcome me, and I thank them. I breathe deeply and stare at the acoustic tile above our heads. "In September of 2001 my mother was killed by her husband. Shot. He was a cop. He disappeared and was found three months later, dead, in New Mexico. He'd killed himself."

When I'm done, their faces haven't changed. Kate thanks me for sharing. "Everybody here understands." She waves at the windows, the dark world outside. "Nobody out there understands, but we do."

Another story, a few announcements, and the meeting ends. Everyone stands and says goodbye. A few people ask if I'm coming back next month, and I say sure. Kate gives me a hug. On the way out I notice that someone has brought baked goods, a tray of brownies sprinkled with sugar and layered with fudge. The pest control lady says she baked them herself and offers me one. I eat it in one bite. She smiles and says to have another, so I do. Only willpower and a vague sense of propriety keep me from taking a third. I'm suddenly ravenous: I want to eat a steak, drink whiskey, fuck a stranger. And I want to get out of here.

I rush down the halls and out the automatic door, across the parking lot to my car, where I sit in the driver's seat with the keys shaking in my hands until the dome light goes off. I watch the others shuffle out in a group, clinging to one another, saying goodbye a half-dozen times, hesitant to leave because they know what waits at home. I want them to heal, to live again, but most of all I want to believe that I'm not one of them.

Three men died in the Gunfight at the O.K. Corral: Billy Clanton and the McLaury brothers, Frank and Tom. Frank was thirty-three at the time of his death, Tom was twenty-eight, and Billy was just nineteen. All three had lived in the area before the silver boom, unlike the Earps, who had come to Tombstone hoping to get rich quick. The McLaury brothers and Billy Clanton associated with outlaws but weren't outlaws themselves, certainly no more so than the Earps, who moonlighted as gamblers and pimps. Accounts of the three men's reputations vary but agree on one thing: their funeral drew the biggest crowd in Tombstone's history.

They're buried at the edge of town, in a shared grave in Boothill, beneath a marker that reads "Murdered in the Streets of Tombstone." Tourists tend to snap a picture and walk on by, searching in vain for the Earps, and I don't blame them. Who wants to see the victims?

TOMBSTONE

Laura comes to visit. I spot her standing on the airport curb in a long skirt and a tank top, new sunglasses and a ponytail, and when I get out of the car and pull her into a hug she smells like soap and perfume, reminding me of a whole world I've forgotten these last few weeks, a cleaner life with her in California. If my mother had lived to meet Laura, she would have called her classy.

We play house, cook dinner, take walks through the neighborhood at night making plans for the future. We're moving in together at the end of the summer, when I get back to San Francisco. We talk about what it'll be like to have our own place, discuss neighborhoods, rents, furniture. Maybe we'll get a dog. I've never cohabitated before, and as a new life forms in my mind, I do my best not to think of the dreams like this I've seen end badly.

Until my mother died, I'd never had a serious girlfriend; afterward, I couldn't be alone. That first date I went on after-

---

ward, with Eliza, my coworker at the college newspaper, turned into a yearlong relationship, the first in a series. I tried different ways of telling the women I dated about my mother. I learned to wait, to choose a private moment, preferably at night—otherwise it lingered for the rest of the day—and I settled on the passive voice, used *killed* instead of *murdered,* didn't specify the method unless they asked, and they usually wouldn't, not right away. I dated one woman for more than a year and never told her the truth.

Things changed once they knew. They wouldn't ask about my mother, wouldn't talk about theirs, wouldn't even say the word *mother.* When we argued, they would watch me warily, like I was some wild animal. I knew what they were afraid of, the same thing I was. I've never touched a woman in anger and I never would. But that's what they all say.

As women came and went, I began to feel like I was living out some kind of prophecy, becoming like my mother, restless and demanding, chasing a delusion of a better life to come. When my last girlfriend before Laura, an Ivy League knockout I'd met in grad school, left me to return to New York, I tried to do what I'd never done after my mother died, what she'd never done at all: learn to live alone. It was hard at first, passing days without speaking, knowing there was nobody to see me brood, but over time I grew to prefer being alone. I began to think maybe I'd never get married, never have kids, never subject myself or anyone else to my family legacy of failed relationships.

Then Laura came along, like a revelation. She knew about my mother, and she knew the risks of loving a man like me, a man so full of rage. But she did it anyway. Since I met her, failure doesn't seem so certain anymore.

After a week in the guesthouse, things get tense. Five hundred square feet, the swamp cooler creaking, the middle of July. A buck ten in the daytime, thunderstorms at night. We spend every moment together, sit on the couch reading and sweating, go to matinées of shitty movies just for the AC. Laura's never been to Arizona and wants to do the tourist thing, but I've always hated tourists, how they gather in herds where their guidebooks tell them to, saying it's not what they expected. Eventually I relent and take her to Tombstone.

Halfway there, we pass a billboard for the O.K. Corral: a man in a black coat and hat, mustached and severe, staring down the barrel of a revolver at us. It's supposed to be Wyatt Earp, although the man on the billboard doesn't look much like him, and he's way too old to be Wyatt in his Tombstone days. Thirty miles away, I'm already throttling the steering wheel, breathing fast. This was a bad idea. I could pull over, turn around, but what would I tell Laura? She wants to see my hometown, the place I talk about so much, and I don't know how to explain why I haven't been back in years, how every time I climb that last long hill into town I feel marked. Everyone there knows me as Debbie's son. They probably wonder why I never go back, probably assume that I think I'm too good. Or maybe they don't care; maybe the town has forgotten. But I doubt it—Tombstone loves a murder.

Tucson is neutral ground, which is one reason I decided to stay there for the summer. But once I cross the Cochise County line, everything reminds me of my mother. On Benson's main drag, the storefront of Ziering's, a mercantile with a wall of exotic candy in jars, run by a gentle old man who took a shine to Mom the first time we went in. Farther down the highway, the feed store where she bought hay, a house where one of her boyfriends lived, the swimming hole outside Saint David we went to in the summer until some kid broke his neck and they shut it down. This county is a minefield of memories.

Finally we top a rise and there it is, on a plateau in the middle of the valley, a cluster of low buildings ringed by bare brown hills: Tombstone. It's not much to look at, and disappoints almost everybody at first sight. The town's early settlers wrote east to report its ugliness; it hasn't gotten prettier since. Tourists used to tell me they were expecting a real ghost town, not paved streets and power lines and so many people.

Some things have changed—the new high school on the edge of town, a new hotel along the highway—but mostly my hometown looks the same. Rental cars cluster in the Boothill parking lot, and a police cruiser sits outside the Circle K. The brown clapboard we lived in on Fremont Street, across from Wyatt Earp's house, is now a real estate office. The original house was a shotgun miner's shack built in the 1880s, since shoddily expanded, all slanting floors and doors that don't close and closets overrun with spiders. I lived there with my mother for a year when I was fourteen. My brother was gone and no man was living with us, and I would sneak out at night and drink and get high and not even try to hide any of it from her, daring her to stop me. I'd hear her crying at night in her room, and I knew it was partly because she felt so alone, and partly because she thought she had lost me to the town she'd grown by then to hate, the town that had already turned her only brother into a hopeless case. One night I saw her through the window, standing in the backyard among the knee-high weeds, holding a hamper of clothes she'd just taken off the line, bathed in white and blue from the Chevron sign across the street, staring blankly into the distance, and she stood there motionless for so long I wondered if I was dreaming or hallucinating, if she was a ghost. I don't fully believe that memory, but it's the image I remember most vividly from that time. If I wanted to show Laura my Tombstone, if I thought anyone else would care or understand, I'd point out our old house and tell her all this.

The sky is low and gray over town, and rain begins to fall as we park on Toughnut Street. Town seems busy for a weekday, the parking lots almost full, but it's the summer, the busy season. We start at the courthouse, where we can see some of the real history before all the bullshit uptown. We do the rounds, the saddle you can take a picture sitting on, the restored courtroom, the gallows yard in back. The original gallows have been replaced with a replica, dangling nooses and all. Only a handful of men were hung here, but the eeriness is unmistakable: it feels like a place where someone died. Visitors speak in whispers in the yard, and nobody stays very long. When I was a kid, my friends and I would play touch football in the front yard of the courthouse, and when the game was done, we'd scale the wall and peek over at the gallows, pretending to see ghosts.

Next is the World's Largest Rosebush, just a block up Toughnut, where for five bucks apiece we enter a courtyard walled off from the street and step from stone to stone through a vast puddle of rainwater beneath a canopy of branches the size of a small house, supported by a latticework of wood and metal pipes, strung with pale yellow bulbs. It's my favorite place in all of Tombstone, the only pure thing in this whole town, the only attraction that doesn't depend on somebody dying. A hundred years ago a man planted a clipping behind his house, and tended it faithfully as it grew. On a day like today, dripping rain slicing the sky into diamonds, it's beautiful. It's a block from the O.K. Corral and gets half the traffic.

The woman behind the ticket counter at the O.K. Corral asks if I want to see the show; they've built an amphitheater next to the scene of the shootout for staging reenactments. I decline. We walk through the gift shop and out the back, taking the opposite route the Earps did—they walked down Fremont, never entering the corral itself. In fact, the gunfight didn't happen at the O.K. Corral; it happened in a vacant lot to the north, between a back alley and what is now the highway. But try putting that on a T-shirt.

In my Tombstone, the O.K. Corral is the least important place on this block. Just across the highway is the house where my friend David lived; I spent a night in his bathroom vomiting and praying to God the first time I got drunk, at thirteen, on straight tequila. Thirty feet east is the Tombstone Marshal's Office, where Ray worked, and where I was read my rights and made to give a statement after the pellet gun incident. To the west is the RV park that my old roommate Joe's family used to own. To the south, past the stucco wall of the amphitheater, is a park with a swing set I used to play on as a kid. If I were here alone, I'd avoid Allen Street altogether, and instead go to the places I remember, to see what's changed or been destroyed, what's been bought and sold. Nothing ever changes in these places, the museums, the tourist attractions: that's the point, to pretend the past can be preserved.

But the diorama of the gunfight *has* changed. I notice it right away, from across the yard: the statues are different somehow. The old ones were bad plaster effigies of the Earps and Clantons, grossly undersized, and the effect was tragicomic, two distant groups of dwarfs battling to the death. The new statues are bigger and closer together, and a low iron fence surrounds them. Animatronic gun arms move up and down on cues from a push-button voice-over. A sign explains the new orientation, claiming that a map of the gunfight has recently been discovered, drawn by Wyatt Earp himself, and that it "resolves a century-long debate over the exact location of the gunfighters." Wyatt drew the map in 1924, forty-three years after the fact. It's reproduced on the sign, a single sheet of paper, boxes and scrawls and Xs for the combatants, an eerily childish diagram of the killing of three men.

For all the attention it gets, the books and movies and daily reenactments, the millions of tourists who've visited the site, the minor controversies about who shot first and who killed whom, and the entire town that lives off its legend, there wasn't much to the Gunfight at the O.K. Corral. Two groups of men in a vacant yard. About thirty shots in about thirty seconds. Three men injured, all from the Earp party: Virgil shot in the leg, Doc's hip grazed by a bullet, and Morgan with a nasty wound across his back. Three men killed: Billy Clanton and both McLaury brothers. Of the men who fought, only Wyatt walked away unscathed.

It's a hell of a thing to wish for, but I wonder how history might be different if Wyatt hadn't been so lucky. If he'd died in the gunfight, he never would've become a legend, and Tombstone would have wound up like all the other crumbling ghost towns dotting the desert around here, abandoned and forgotten. My mother would never have come here to see the O.K. Corral, never decided to move, never met Ray, and so on. I like to imagine that she'd be living in some trailer by the beach, riding horses in the surf, watching sunsets. But she probably would have wound up in some other nowhere town, with some other man, who would have hurt her in some other way.

As we're leaving, I spot a plaque tucked away in a corner of the lot, where it's easy to miss. It's a memorial to the McLaury brothers, Frank and Tom, who fell within sight of each other on Fremont Street, both gutshot and dying. The plaque was donated by their descendants. "One owes respect to the living," it says. "But to the dead, one owes nothing but the truth."

Against my better judgment, I take Laura to Madame Mustache, the gift shop my mother owned. We wander through the displays, shot glasses and coffee mugs and Christmas ornaments, refrigerator magnets and T-shirts and toy guns, all sitting on shelves my mother built by hand. The old-time photo booth in back is open. I suggest that we get our picture taken. I'm joking, but Laura agrees. What the hell.

A reedy, balding man with a thin mustache emerges from the back room and fits us with costumes. I choose Morgan Earp, and Laura is a dance-hall girl, although all the costumes look pretty much the same, gunfighters and whores. The photographer's fingers are delicate and pale, dirty-nailed and reeking of smoke, and they tremble as he buttons my vest. He looks a lot like Fredo from the Godfather movies, and acts the part, talks a lot and seems nervous, as if he's waiting for some disaster. He hands me a nickel-plated replica revolver and tells me how to pose.

When we're done, he rings us up and I realize that I don't have enough cash to pay for the pictures. Laura doesn't have any either, so I hand him my credit card. After he swipes it, he pinches its edge and peers at the name.

"Are you related to the St. Germains here?"

"She was my mother."

He looks at me as if he's seeing me for the first time. His eyes are bloodshot and sad. "And Cool Breeze?"

"His name's Tom. He was my uncle."

He reaches across the counter to shake my hand. His is cold and bony.

"I'm sorry," he says.

"Thanks."

The receipt is printing. Laura feigns interest in a rack of

feathered boas. The man tells me his name and says he used to work with my mother at one of her jobs. He says how good of a boss she was, how well she treated her employees. I don't know about that; she made me work at this store when I was in middle school, paid me minimum wage, scheduled me for weekend mornings. The photo man continues. "And then she met"—his fingers bend into quotes, and his lips curl into a sneer—"that *cop*."

"Yep." I sign the receipt.

"At first they seemed so happy. But then . . . well, he just lost it. It was sad." This conversation is always the same: here comes the moral. "I guess you just never know."

I grab the photos. "You take care."

Five minutes later I'm speeding past the city limit sign.

We stop for dinner in Benson at a diner with a spinning display of pies and little jukeboxes on the tables. As we sit down, I remember that my mother always ordered the roast beef dinner here, and I wish we'd kept driving. We're the only customers. When the silence gets to be too much, Laura says she's sorry about what happened earlier.

"We didn't have to go to Tombstone," she says.

"Now you say that."

"I didn't know. . . ." When she's upset, when she's guilty, when she thinks she's hurt someone, Laura's voice goes low and hoarse, and it usually strikes a chord inside me. But not today.

"What did you expect?"

The waitress delivers our food and flees. We eat in silence and drive home. Opening the guesthouse door unleashes a blast of heat, and right away I want to escape, go find a bar with air-conditioning and sit alone among other people. Laura's probably thinking the same thing. We've been living like this for a week, sharing a hot and confined space with only each other for company, and already we're restless and trapped, irritable, picking fights and having doubts.

My mother and Ray lived like this for two years.

We spend Laura's last night in town making up and making plans. She'll go back to San Francisco and find us an apartment, and in a few weeks, when this is over, I'll join her. I imagine our first place together: bare floors, empty cabinets, a clean slate.

But later, as she sleeps beside me, I lie awake, watching the ceiling fan whirl, listening for suspicious sounds in the night, reaching down to touch the handle of the machete I found in the guesthouse closet so I know it's still where I put it, under the bed, in arm's reach. We can talk about the future all we want, other lives in other places, maybe marriage, maybe kids. But I can't imagine the future when I'm surrounded by the past: police reports, videos and pictures, a box of my mother's things. The desert. The Beast. The plaque for the victims at the O.K. Corral: *to the dead, one owes nothing but the truth*.

CONSEQUENCES

O n my twenty-eighth birthday, a package from the
Cochise County sheriff comes in the mail, a padded
envelope that weighs a few pounds. I cut it open and
dump the contents onto the coffee table: a stack of paper and
a plastic bag with an orange "biohazard" sticker.

The bag contains two smaller bags. A paper sack, stapled
shut and also labeled "biohazard," holds only a pink camera
with no film inside. The police might have taken the film as
evidence, or it might have been empty when they found it.
Either way, it does me no good.

The other bag is made of thick plastic and is also labeled
"biohazard." My mother's name is misspelled in black marker
across the top, next to a case number and a red X in a red circle,
the significance of which isn't clear. It contains jewelry the
medical examiner took off of her body: a bracelet, a necklace,
and a few rings. The bracelet is gold, engraved with a floral
pattern and the word *Kepi,* her first name in Hawaiian. She had

it made in Maui when we were there on vacation. Her airborne ring is the only one I recognize, also gold, with wings around an open parachute and a diamond set above the canopy. I never saw her take it off. Two of the others, a matching set, must be the engagement and wedding rings Ray gave her. The necklace is braided and gold, and holds a silver cross still flecked with her dried blood.

I gave her a ring once. When I was a kid, my friends and I would fish between the cracks of the boardwalk along Allen Street, digging out coins with chewing gum stuck to the end of straws. One day I found a gold band with the word *love* on its face and a small diamond in the middle of the *o*. I gave it to her. I wonder where it is now, if she lost it, if I left it behind in the trailer.

The stack of paper is an inch thick, held together by a binder clip. It's everything I asked for, all the sections that were missing from my copy of the police report on my mother's death, as well as a copy of another police report, about the discovery of another body.

Caballo Lake sits in southwestern New Mexico, surrounded by national forest and the missile range where the atomic bomb debuted, a few miles downriver from Truth or Consequences. The state park facilities—campgrounds, a boat launch, cactus gardens, and a ranger station—are sandwiched into a strip of desert between the lake and I-25, overlooking the western shore. I arrive on a Sunday afternoon. I had never known exactly where Ray's body was found until I read the report, and now I want to see the place where he died.

The park is nearly empty, just a handful of weekenders packing up and towing their boats back to Albuquerque and El Paso. The lake recedes ahead, jade green and calm, and the Caballo Mountains rise abruptly from the far shore. Out on the water a few boats trail ribbons of froth, stragglers getting in one more lap around the lake, dragging skiers or wakeboarders or, if they're anything like my family was, some sunburned kid in an inner tube. We used to take our leaky old ski boat to lakes like this one all over the Southwest—Patagonia, Powell, Mead, Havasu, Alamo—and on Sunday afternoons with the sun getting low and a long drive home ahead, I'd beg my mother to stay out just a little longer, and she would.

At the ranger station, I buy a day pass and decide not to ask where the body was found in 2001. The girl who sells me the pass is too young to have worked here that long, and even if she has, she might not know which body I mean. In the late nineties there was a rash of floaters in a reservoir a few miles north of here called Elephant Butte. Then a woman was spotted running down a nearby street wearing only a dog collar and a chain. Police followed her directions to a trailer park and found a torture chamber. The man who owned the place, David Parker Ray, called it his "toy box." Investigators said he might have killed dozens of people. He pled guilty to some of the charges, said that he was sorry. He was sentenced to more than two hundred years in prison, but died of a heart attack less than a year later.

When I did an Internet search for David Parker Ray, wanting to see what he looked like, I found a picture of a New Mexico state policeman walking his accomplice out of a courtroom. I recognized the policeman's name in the photo's caption. A few months after it was taken, the same policeman, Agent Bishop, came to Caballo Lake to investigate a death.

After the gunfight, after Wyatt's brothers were shot in revenge, and after the famed Vendetta ride in which he killed the three men he thought responsible, warrants were issued for his arrest and President Arthur threatened to impose martial law on Cochise County. Wyatt fled to New Mexico. He stopped briefly in Silver City, then Albuquerque, then moved on to Colorado. He thought he would be pardoned for his crimes, and planned to go back to Tombstone eventually; he wasn't, and he didn't. He wound up, like many former Tombstoners, in San Francisco.

A few months after Wyatt left, one of his old enemies, a mysterious figure named Johnny Ringo, turned up dead at the base of a tree in eastern Arizona with a revolver in his hand and a hole in his head. It was ruled a suicide, and it probably was. But that didn't stop writers from claiming decades later that Wyatt had snuck back across the border and murdered one last man.

After he killed my mother, when everyone was looking for him, Ray left Arizona, but nobody knows where he went. Freeney followed the few leads he had. He called Ray's exwife, who put him in touch with relatives. Ray's mother and stepfather lived in Florida and said they hadn't talked to him in some time. His grandparents in Montana said it had been about a year. They couldn't believe he'd done something like that.

His family claimed not to have seen him. He never had many friends as far as anyone could tell. He didn't have much money, and he would have known his bank accounts and phone calls were being monitored. But he'd been traveling the country on and off for the last two years, living hand to mouth, finding remote places to camp. He'd been in the Marine Corps. He wasn't very smart, but he was resourceful. He lasted almost three months.

On December 9, 2001, Agent Bishop of the New Mexico State Police got a call from his sergeant around noon: a ranger in Caballo was reporting a body. He must have thought of David Parker Ray, his victims that were never found. But this wasn't a floater, and it wasn't a woman. The ranger had found a dead man in a truck.

Bishop responded to the scene. En route, dispatch told him they'd done a plate check. The vehicle was registered to Deborah St. Germain and Duane Raymont Hudson, of Tombstone. He arrived at the scene to find a red Ford pickup parked by a stand of mesquite and four other agents already there, standing in a clearing with the ranger. As Bishop approached and circled the truck, he noted the make and model and plate, the empty water tank in back, mud on the tires, the tinted windows open a couple of inches, the sunscreen blocking his view through the windshield, and the cell phone antenna jutting above the rear window, its cable disconnected. A toolbox in the truck bed was unlocked and held nothing of interest. In the dirt around the truck he saw no tire tracks that seemed related, no footprints other than those made by the rangers. He smelled a strong odor coming from inside the truck.

The left rear door was locked. Bishop peered through the window and saw a body on its back, partially covered by a sheet. He couldn't tell the gender and he couldn't see the face, only the arms: the right lay alongside the body, and the left hung down to the floorboard. On the center console between the front seats he saw an open spiral notebook with writing on the page, but couldn't read the message. A driver's license and a wedding band sat on top of the note. The keys were on the seat.

The report includes a photocopy of Ray's driver's license. The picture copied poorly: half his smiling face is dark, the rest white and ghastly. I remembered wrong: his eyes were blue, not brown. He was five-eight, a hundred and sixty-five pounds, thirty-five at the time of his death.

It also includes a copy of the suicide note. It's hard to read. His handwriting is sloppy and strangely angled, a few mistakes scribbled over. The note is spattered with black dots of various sizes, blood and brain matter. As near as I can tell, it says:

> I can no longer endure the pessimistic and fatalistic demeanor of my life. Nor can I continue to live a life of falsehoods and lies. The constant negative attitude has caused so much mental strain and anguish that I have reached a point of no return.
>
> I have once again failed in life. I failed in my Marine Corps career, my law enforcement career, my first marriage and fatherhood and now my second marriage.
>
> My actions have set my fate and destiny and also expedited them.
>
> I have ruined many lives and I am sorry.

The first time I read it, I thought: what a crock of shit. He doesn't admit what he did, doesn't use any of the words: *murder, wife, mother.* He doesn't even say her name. Instead, he says he's sorry. On the second read I noticed the details. The inflated diction: *pessimistic, fatalistic, expedited;* I guess he had been reading. The wire spine of the notebook is on the right; he began the note on the back of a page. What was on the front, the rough draft?

And the signature: Duane R. Hudson. Duane. I never heard him called it. To me he was Ray. But in the last words he ever wrote, he didn't think enough of that name to spell it out—it's just an initial, just a crooked *R.* Did he always go by Ray, or was he once Duane, in some previous life? Did he become Duane when he became a murderer? When he thought of himself, what name did he use?

Past the ranger station there's an empty parking lot and a ring of deserted campsites. Halfway down the hill to the boat launch, I stop at the bathrooms, where a scratched Plexiglas display holds a map of Caballo Lake and a bunch of warnings about drowning and snakes. The report says only that Ray was found in a remote area of the park, but this is a minor state park in rural New Mexico: it's all remote area.

The day is bright and hot, the sky vast and blue and clear save for a rim of clouds on the north horizon. A minute out of the car, sweat rolls down my ribs, and the sun off the water hurts my eyes even through sunglasses. The smells of shit and chemicals waft from the bathrooms. Farther down the hill, a half-dozen empty boat trailers lie nosedown in a line by the launch. From there a faint road turns off into a flat stretch of desert that overlooks the shore, which is marked on the map as primitive campgrounds. I get back in the car, crank the air-conditioning, and head that way.

The road is rutted dirt, bordered by cacti. It crosses shallow washes and winds through stands of brush. Except for a cinder-block bathroom, this part of the park is empty desert, dirt roads that cross and circle back, leading nowhere.

I stop in a clearing and pull the report out of my bag. It contains forty-eight grainy images—copies of copies, tawdry and unreal. The first few photos show the truck from a distance, partially hidden by a mass of black branches and a web of shadows. It's impossible to tell where it was, which stand of mesquite, which clearing along which of these roads, if it was even in this part of the park. I flip through the pages, looking for clues. The camera moves closer, the truck emerging, that familiar Ford, the chrome toolbox in the bed, the empty water tank that in the picture is just a plash of washed-out white. A chrome Jesus fish on the tailgate above an Arizona license plate—the old white-on-maroon—in a chrome plate holder that says: *The More Men I Meet . . . the More I Like My Horse.*

The next picture, the front of the truck, its rectangular grille, the orange running lights on top of the cab, brings back a night one summer just before I left home. A monsoon storm split the sky with lightning and flooded the washes around our trailer. I was in a hurry, just off work, driving home to shower before I went to meet my girlfriend, and I got stuck trying to cross a gully where the water was deeper than it looked. My truck sank to its axle in the sand. The water was above the exhaust pipe and rising. If I didn't get it out soon, the truck would be swamped, maybe even swept away, wind up battered and waterlogged a quarter mile downstream, like the cars immigrants abandoned in washes. I stood in the pouring rain, drenched, starting to panic, and saw our trailer lights flickering in the distance behind sheets of rain. I ran, hoping somebody was home.

I crashed through the door dripping water and tracking mud, startling my mother, who wouldn't listen to what I was saying, just kept asking if I was all right. Ray understood; he went and got his keys, and we climbed into the Ford. Those big headlights fell on the front end of my truck rising from the gully like the prow of a foundering ship. Ray didn't ask why I'd tried to cross it, didn't scold me or complain about the rain soaking his shirt and dripping from the brim of his hat. He just grabbed a chain out of the toolbox and handed me one end, said to make sure to hook it to the frame, not the bumper, got back in the Ford and pulled me out. Five minutes later we were back home, the trucks in the driveway and us warm and dry inside, sitting at the dinner table, drinking tea, watching the flat plain of desert outside flood, cracking jokes about my driving. Was that the life of falsehoods and lies he mentioned in his note?

Agent Bishop took the notebook into evidence, along with the license and Ray's wedding ring. Ray had left the ring atop the note in a gesture he must have thought profound, but it only makes me wonder why he waited three months to take it off. Bishop unlocked and opened the truck's rear door. The body was male, decomposed, stretched out on the seat, head hanging backward and to the left. A handgun lay on the floorboard near the left hand, a Browning with a round in the chamber and eight in the clip. Bishop noted a strong putrefying odor and maggots in varying stages of development on and around the body. He took samples to help determine a time of death.

The medical investigators arrived, pronounced the man dead, and removed his body from the truck, laying it on a blanket on the ground. They located an entry wound in the left temple and an exit wound in the right. A pair of holes in the truck's rear seat showed where the bullet had passed through, but Bishop couldn't locate the slug itself, only the spent casing, which he placed into evidence along with the gun and live ammunition. Bishop photographed the body before the medical investigators took it away.

The first picture of Ray shows only the outline of his boots in the darkened cab of the truck; he died with them on. The next photo shows Ray's body lying in shadow, the sun slanting through the open door of the truck and onto the top of his bald head. Bishop is a worthy photographer: he withholds what I want to see, keeps me waiting, creates suspense. The next few photos show the gun, resting on a piece of paper on the ground: a Browning Fabrique Nationale Model 1922 in .32 caliber, an awkward-looking automatic manufactured in Belgium, a slight variant of the gun that killed Archduke Ferdinand. It was developed for the Yugoslav army after World War I and used throughout eastern Europe for most of the twentieth century. Hundreds of thousands of 1922s exist, but the serial number listed in the report indicates, according to various online resources, that Ray's pistol was manufactured in 1941, under occupation, for the Nazis. I wonder if he knew that.

I turn the page again and there he is, lying on a blanket in the dirt, badly decomposed and yet still somehow recognizable. Ray's body is shrunken, his head pressed against his left shoulder, hands hanging gnarled near his waist. It looks as if he died in pain, and I hope he did, but his twisted body is probably an effect of weeks spent decomposing in the desert.

The next picture shows his face, but between the decay and the bad copy, I can only make out his right eye socket and cheek, a mess of matted hair and beard, a glimpse of teeth; the rest is hidden by a sinewy darkness. He looks almost penitent, but that's probably wishful thinking. A face like that can't convey anything but regret.

Agent Bishop saved his masterpiece for late in the sequence: roll three, photograph six: *close-up of left hand of Duane Hudson.* The others are evidence, but this is art. The shot shows Ray's left hand, swollen knuckles and cracked skin, nails long and clawlike because the beds around them have dried and receded. Halfway closed, his hand is as it was when he died, letting go of something it once held. The framing tells the story: his hand slightly right of center, his belt buckle to the left, a swarm of maggots gathered on the front of his pants at the bottom edge. In the upper right corner, past the white edge of the blanket, a triangle of dust. And in the middle, drawing my eye, his trigger finger, still human, still half bent.

I once asked Ray if he'd ever shot anybody. It was soon after I met him, before he moved in. We'd just finished lunch at my mother's restaurant, the tablecloth between us strewn with tomato chunks and bits of tortilla, and he was about to go back to work. I glanced at the gun holstered on his hip. It didn't bother me—half the men in Tombstone wore guns, and at least he didn't have the whole costume, ten-gallon hat and duster, chaps and spurs, shell belts, all that shit. But when a person wears a gun, it works its way into conversations.

"No," he said. "I've come close."

"In the war?"

He took a drink of tea and wiped his mouth with a napkin. "No, I didn't see any combat, just hauled stuff around. It wasn't much of a war."

He said it had happened when he was a cop in Huachuca City. He got a call for a domestic disturbance out in Whetstone. It wasn't his jurisdiction, but he went anyway, because the county sheriffs would have taken hours to respond, if they even bothered. In the middle of telling the story, Ray picked up his pipe and began to load it with tobacco from a bag. He said he'd responded to the scene, a trailer at the end of a dirt road, and a man came walking out onto the steps.

Ray leaned toward me.

"He's got a baseball bat in his hands, and he looks crazy, like he's on meth."

"Jesus."

"Yeah. Bad news." He held a disposable lighter to the bowl

217

of his pipe and flicked it a few times before it lit. Later I would suggest that we get him a torch lighter for Christmas. He continued his story, puffing smoke.

"I tell him to drop the bat. He tells me to get the fuck off his property. I hear a woman yelling inside." Ray was nailing all the pauses, drawing it out. I could tell he'd told this story before.

"I tell him again. He doesn't drop it. So I draw my sidearm." Ray made a gun with his fingers and pointed it at me. I looked at the real one on his hip.

"Can you shoot somebody in that situation?"

"If I thought I was in danger."

"But would you?"

"I don't know," Ray said. "He dropped the bat."

He went on to tell me that he'd put the man in cuffs, taken him to the station, saved the woman. Mom came by to check on us and listened to the happy ending. When Ray was done, he got up from the table, kissed her goodbye, nodded to me, and went back to protecting and serving. Mom lingered with me at the table, listening to the house mariachi tune his guitar.

Ray's story stuck with me. I wondered what had happened when the man got out of jail. Maybe he'd gone back and pleaded for forgiveness and cried crocodile tears, promising it would never happen again, like Max used to. Or, if he was a different kind of man, he came home and picked up the bat and finished what he'd started. Either way, I imagined the woman was still there, waiting, because that's the way it always goes.

Ray's body went to Albuquerque for identification. A tow truck came and took the Ford away. Bishop left the scene and returned to his office in T or C, where he called the Cochise

County Sheriff's Office and spoke to Freeney. He asked for my mother's contact information, so he could tell her that he'd found her husband. Freeney filled him in.

Freeney told Bishop a slightly different story from the one he'd told me. He said Ray never had a warrant out for his arrest because there wasn't enough evidence—no witnesses, no murder weapon—and he said that Ray had a history of domestic violence with his former wife.

Freeney asked him about the murder weapon, the Beretta, if he'd found it in the truck. Bishop said he'd look again in the morning.

First thing the next day, Bishop talked to Ray's ex-wife, who helped positively identify the body by describing his tattoos. She said that after he left Arizona, Ray had crossed the Canadian border and may have stopped in Montana. Either Bishop didn't ask how she knew that, or he didn't record her answer.

Bishop went to the towing company to search the truck, and collected forty-nine photographs, various documents, three pistol holsters, a box of .32 ammunition, a cell phone, a pink 35 mm camera, and four road atlases, but no gun. He sent the evidence to Freeney. For some unfathomable reason, all of it was destroyed except for the pink camera. Only when I read the report did I realize that Ray had their cell phone the whole time he was on the run. Why didn't I think to call it? What would he have said? What would I have said?

Two days later, Bishop talked to the medical investigators. They'd received Ray's fingerprints from the Arizona Department of Public Safety, which had them on file from his time as a police officer. The prints matched. The remains were positively identified as Duane Raymont Hudson.

My mother had left me the truck in her will. She'd written that I should sell it to pay for college, since I wouldn't be getting her VA checks once she died. After Ray's body was found, I got the towing company's phone number and called; I didn't particularly want the truck, but I wasn't going to let Ray take that, too. The man who answered was gruff and annoyed. He said I'd have to prove ownership. I said I could. He said, with far too much satisfaction in his tone, that there would be storage fees.

"You're going to charge me storage fees for a stolen vehicle?"

"Somebody's got to pay."

I asked him how much. He said he'd get back to me, then tried another angle. "It's in no shape to drive. You'll have to put it on a flatbed and tow it. The smell . . . You'll have to replace the whole interior."

I made him list exactly what would need to be replaced. His voice rose into a whine. I knew it didn't matter—I didn't have a flatbed trailer, and what was I going to do with a spare truck that smelled like death and reminded me of my dead mother and murdering stepfather every time I saw it? But as he went on and on, talking about odors in the plastic, maggots, dried blood, the rage bloomed in my chest. I told him to get the truck ready, that I'd be there in the morning. Then I hung up, threw the phone across the room, and screamed into a pillow until I was out of breath. That night I fell asleep fantasizing about walking into the towing company and opening fire.

For a fleeting moment as I turn out of the park, I think of that man on the phone. It's not far to Truth or Consequences. The name of the company is in the police report. I could go find him. I could drive on. The choice I make every day: what kind of man to be?

HIGH LONESOME

I stop in Hatch for gas. Every small town in the Southwest claims to be famous for something: Hatch is a chile town. Along the road hang signs for chile, red or green, fresh or frozen, strung in bunches, cooked in stew. The town itself is run-down and half deserted, a lot like the parts of Tombstone outside the tourist district, a lot like any small town around here. Driving through, I have the same daydreams that come whenever I see a place this far away from anywhere: I want to move here and start a new life where nobody knows me, renovate an old house, sit on the porch and watch the sunset, lean against a pump at the gas station and gossip with the locals. It's pure romantic bullshit, an elitist fantasy, the simple life. I ought to know better, ought to remember how it feels to live in a place like this, the grinding poverty, the lack of opportunity, all the kinds of self-defeat—alcohol, drugs, gossip—the gnawing fear that you haven't gotten away from the world, it's gotten away from you.

Decades after he left Arizona, Wyatt Earp wanted a simpler life. San Francisco soured on him when he was accused of fixing a heavyweight fight. Rumors followed him to the Klondike, where he was falsely reported to have been knocked out by a midget in a barroom brawl in Dawson. In Los Angeles he was accused of cardsharping and arrested for vagrancy. Every few years the Tombstone stories would appear in the newspapers again, fantastically distorted.

Wyatt bought a mine out in the Mojave Desert, a stone's throw from Arizona, and spent his winters there, prospecting. It never made him much money, but at least nobody bothered him; out there he didn't have to be Wyatt Earp. He called his mine the Happy Days.

The day after my mother's body was found, at around one in the afternoon, as the medical examiner was making his first incisions, as my brother's phone began to ring, and as I rode my bike home, a pair of detectives were leaving the scene of the crime. They had just finished taking measurements of the trailer and outlying structures, and had talked to an officer from the Department of Agriculture who was trying to find my mother's horses. The detectives tried to interview the nearest neighbors, but only one was home, the mother of a girl I went to grade school with. She said she'd lived there for twelve years, but she didn't know my mother and Ray. People out there mostly kept to themselves. She hadn't heard any gunshots, hadn't seen anything of interest. The detectives thanked her and left.

After that, they went to Bob and Connie's. The transcript of their conversation, all twenty-two pages, is in the envelope Freeney sent me. The detectives began by asking them to go over recent events.

Bob said my mother and Ray had spent the night at their place on Sunday, September 16. He didn't say why, but they often stayed at Bob and Connie's when they didn't want to drive home in the dark, when it was too cold in their trailer, or when they wanted company besides each other. They left Monday, promising to return Wednesday to help Bob feed his horses—he'd just turned seventy-eight, he explained, and his legs were acting up, and Connie had to go to California for a couple of days. It was the last time they saw my mother and Ray alive.

Wednesday came and they didn't show. Bob fed the horses himself. Around noon he still hadn't heard from them, so he drove out to Gleeson to check. At the property, Chance was running loose and the horses were in the corral, but the truck was gone. He drove back home and called Connie. They agreed that it was strange. Bob kept paging my mother and calling her cell phone but didn't get an answer. He decided to drive out there again.

At the property, he went to check on the horses, but Chance wouldn't stop carrying on. Bob went and tried the trailer door, thinking maybe they kept the dog food in there. It was un-locked, so he went inside. He saw my mother on the bed, flat on her face, with her arm like this—his gesture is not described in the transcript—and not wearing any clothes. He thought she was asleep, so he yelled at her a few times, but she didn't move. He went over and touched her foot. It was cold as ice. He didn't see any blood, but that foot seemed awful stiff. He looked closer and saw a little blood right up there on her shoulder. He said he just looked at her for a minute, and then he got in his truck to go find the marshal.

Hours pass on the highway as I drive back to Arizona. The roadside is a panorama of the West. A gas station decays on a frontage road. Strip malls signal the edge of Deming. The boarded hotels of Lordsburg wait for their coup de grâce: a bulldozer, a match. Just past the Arizona border is a sign for the highway to Portal, where Nabokov spent a summer revising *Speak, Memory* and chasing butterflies. Outside Willcox the blue-and-yellow billboards begin, advertising *The Thing?*, a Mystery of the Desert housed in a truck stop near Texas Canyon. My mother took us to see it once, when we were moving to Tombstone; it was the first place we stopped in Arizona. But I don't remember what the Thing is.

I turn south off of I-10 onto a deserted two-lane highway. Abandoned mining equipment sits halfway up a mountainside, fenced off and rusting. Flashing signs warn me to slow down for a Border Patrol checkpoint. A power plant looms gray against the steely sky ahead. I reach for the stereo knob to search through the static, and look up to see the black eyes of a doe peering through my windshield. I swerve; she springs away; I miss her by inches, watch her leap over a fence into a field, and imagine a foal out there, huddled and afraid, waiting for her to return. To the south, in Mexico, a blue range of mountains basks in the sun, but here in the valley it's getting dark. A storm is coming.

The detectives asked Bob and Connie if they'd noticed any problems the last time they saw my mother and Ray. Bob said no. Connie said she'd thought something was wrong, that they didn't seem to want to go home. Bob added something else, but the transcript records it as inaudible. Later in the interview, Connie said that my mother had told her that morning that she needed to take Ray out of her will. I don't remember her will leaving anything to Ray. She might have changed it;

maybe that's what they fought about the day she died. Maybe Connie's memory was wrong. Maybe mine is.

Connie and Bob mentioned that my mother had hurt herself repeatedly in the weeks before she died. She once came to their house limping, saying a horse had stepped on her foot. Shortly before her death, she fell into a fire. She had cleaned out the storage shed on their property and was burning papers in the fire pit, and when she went to get the hose to put out the fire, she tripped and fell backward into the flames. Connie said she wondered, how in the devil can you do that? The detectives asked if there was any indication that Ray had pushed her. They said no.

But afterward my mother had nightmares about it, Connie said, nightmares about burning up. She was distraught. She took down the fire pit.

In the days after her death, writing in a journal every night, I tried in vain to remember the last time I saw my mother. It must not have been long before her death, but it wouldn't come back to me, the last time I hugged her, the last vision of her walking out a door. All these years later, Connie's words in the transcript summon a glimpse: my mother in our living room, wincing and hardly able to walk, telling the story of her burning. She seemed so diminished, so much weaker than the mother I had grown to expect, and I worried that she was falling apart, that her and Ray's vagrant life was unraveling. I felt sorry for her, but a small part of me was glad, thinking she had finally learned some kind of lesson.

That might have happened. She visited us whenever she was in Tucson, and she could have come by our house after she left the hospital. But if it's true, why didn't I remember until now?

At the turn for Gleeson, graffiti on a boarded store window: TIMBUKTU. A sign says Gleeson is eleven miles, Tombstone twenty-seven. I stomp on the gas pedal—cops don't come out here—and roll down the windows. The air is thick and moist and rich and smells like dirt and greasewood. I stop and stand in the road to piss, watching the horizon ahead, green and gray and purple, the hills and the light and the gathering clouds. On the far side of Gleeson rain is already falling, dark wisps descending from the sky. I'm heading right for it.

Warning signs appear: *Flash Flood Area, No Trespassing, Rattlesnake Crafts Ahead*. My cell phone loses signal. I enter Gleeson, what's left of it, a few decrepit houses and a graveyard, a crumbling jail that's on the market. The landscape looks familiar—grassland threaded with scrub, mine derricks dotting the hills—but the landmarks are all wrong. I thought the road through Gleeson was dirt, but it's paved; it turns to dirt past the far edge of town. I remember the rattlesnake store as a roadside adobe shack, but the sign now points down a driveway toward a new house in the distance.

My car clatters over a cattle guard and onto washboard dirt. I thought I'd remember how to find my mother's property, but I don't. It's been a long time, and there are no addresses out here. The police report says it's between two mile markers. I just passed the first.

On the side of the road a freshly graded driveway runs under a steel arch that says High Lonesome Ranch Estates, an ambitious name for a spread of empty lots. A For Sale sign, an empty flyer bin, and No Trespassing signs in English and Spanish hang from the fence below. Power lines run parallel to the road; were there power lines before?

I pass the second marker, turn around, double back.

The detectives asked Connie and Bob about guns. Bob said Ray had guns, he didn't know what kind. Connie said Ray had told them that since the World Trade Center, he didn't go anywhere without guns. He kept them in the truck, loaded. He was just waiting for somebody to try to come onto their property; he was very adamant about that. She also mentioned that one of Debbie's boys had given her a small gun, she didn't know what kind, it was a couple of Christmases ago.

The detectives asked about my brother and me, whether we knew. Connie said she had just gotten off the phone with Josh. She'd wanted us to know before the rumors started; she was sure it would be a big gossip item in town. Bob asked why we hadn't been told sooner. The detectives said they were trying to play catch-up.

Connie volunteered that she hadn't felt good about Debbie's mental state the last time she saw her. There was something between her and Ray that made Connie uneasy. But she had never seen them have an argument. They were together constantly, she said, to the point of . . .

Always together, Bob said.

They would take a shower together, get haircuts together, they were constantly together. I love my husband, Connie said, but I wouldn't want to be with him 24/7, the way they were. It was hard to talk to Debbie without Ray around.

Again Connie returned to the last time she'd seen my mother, the haunting sense that something was wrong. She sat right there and I looked at her face, she said, and I've known Debbie for a lot of years. Then Connie said something about the last few months, but most of it is marked inaudible. She said my mother needed money, that she was concerned about her brother and his kids.

The detectives asked about Uncle Tom, where he lived, his full name, whether he knew what had happened to his sister.

Connie said he'd found out somehow and come out to their house, wanting to know if they had a telephone number. She said whose phone number he wanted, but it's marked inaudible. I wonder if it was mine.

Bob told the detectives what he knew about Tom, most of which is recorded as inaudible. He said Tom had been an alcoholic for a while.

But Debbie was very proud of him, Connie said.

Very proud of him, Bob said.

The last pictures my mother took were of her brother's sons, Sean and Eric, at the property near Gleeson. She must have brought them for a visit right before she died. In one, Ray holds a dead rattlesnake by its head in a snare, dangling the body so the boys could touch its skin, feel the scales. Another shows him skinning it on a flat board. I have a few pictures of Ray with snakes; he must have killed a lot of them. Ray's face is shaded or obscured in every picture of him: by his cowboy hat, by overexposure, by time.

In another photo, my cousin Eric stares through binoculars at the camera. The trailer looms above him, the open window she was facing when Ray fired the first shot. I was wrong, and so were the cops: the trailer's not an Airstream, it's an old Nomad.

The last few pictures she took have nobody in them, only the desert, a hummingbird at a feeder. The final one is mostly dirt, a line of rocks, the trunks of two mesquites, a blur in the corner that might be the bird flying away.

It might not be the last picture. She might have left me a clue, and I just didn't find it. I didn't know how to use her camera, and when I opened it, some of the film was exposed. Then I waited years to have the film developed, let it sit in boxes, on a litany of to-do lists. I didn't see the pictures until recently, and they were disappointing, as by then I knew they would be. There are no clues left, no mystery to solve. I know what happened. I just don't know why.

Halfway between the mile markers noted in the report, two paths lead south from the main road. I passed by them the first time because neither looks familiar, but one of them must be it. Both run dimly through the tall grass for a hundred yards, then crest a rise and disappear. No buildings in sight. The one on the left heads straight, due southwest, and sees regular use—the tracks are wide, no weeds between them. The one on the right winds roughly south, faint and overgrown. I take the one on the right, but not because it's less traveled; it climbs the spine of a rise and offers a better view of the surroundings, and if anyone else is around, I want to see them first. The hair on my arms prickles. Showing up unannounced and uninvited to a stranger's land out here is a good way to get shot.

The steering wheel jerks as my car's tires drop in and out of ruts. I think of the spare I don't have; I got a flat months ago and never replaced it. When I lived in Arizona, I drove trucks. Now I have a city car that sits low to the ground, the worst kind of vehicle for this terrain. If I get stuck, it'll mean a fifteen-mile walk in the rain and a bitch of a towing bill, and that's the best case. The road ahead narrows and twists, drops down a rocky hill.

A quarter mile in, I can't see anything but a lot of empty land. My mother's place wasn't this far off the main road. I turn around.

The last time I spoke to my mother, we talked about the World Trade Center. It was a few days after the attacks, a few days before she died, and I don't remember much of what we said.

On the 11th, she had watched on Bob and Connie's TV as the second plane flew into the tower again and again, becoming a ball of flame, and every time she hoped it might end differently. When she'd heard about the plane in Pennsylvania, she'd worried about Philly, about her parents. She'd had plans for that day, but instead they all just sat on the couch, watching.

She said that Ray was worked up, kept saying a war was coming. She didn't say how Bob reacted, but I bet he wasn't as excited. Bob had served in World War II, Korea, and Vietnam, although he didn't talk about it. Ray had driven a truck in Desert Storm. He talked about it.

My mother was glad not to be in the army anymore; back then she'd always worried that something like this would happen and she'd get deployed, away from us. We talked about terrorists, about fear, about the possibility of more attacks. But mostly we talked about how awful it was, all those people, their families, can you imagine?

We changed the subject, talked about the future. We did that a lot. What I was going to study, what I was going to be, what she was going to do next. She'd just turned forty-four. Money was tight, for both of us, but that would figure itself out. It always had. She and Ray were planning to build a house out on the property, had been doing research about rammed-earth buildings. You did all the work yourself; she liked that idea. By the end she sounded just like she always did, optimistic, convinced that it would all work out. We said goodbye. I'd like to think I told her that I loved her, but I'm not sure I did.

Maybe Connie was right; maybe something was wrong. Maybe my mother had a sense of what was coming. I didn't notice anything out of the ordinary, but she might have fooled me. You never know what a person's capable of.

As the interview went on, Connie and Bob mentioned the World Trade Center repeatedly. The first time they tried to call my mother was on Tuesday, a week after the attacks, and the transcript records a cryptic remark of Bob's: *I told Connie for sure, (inaudible) the World Trade Center (inaudible) about that you know, (inaudible) something like that. . . .* When asked about alcohol, Connie and Bob said that my mother hardly drank at all, and that Ray drank some, not excessively, but *he likes to drink in times like this. . . .*

In the closing pages of the transcript, more and more of the conversation is marked as inaudible. Maybe their voices tired. Maybe the recorder's batteries were dying. Maybe the person transcribing it got lazy, and thought it wouldn't matter.

The detectives asked if they've heard from Ray. Everything Bob said from that point on, the entire last page, is marked inaudible. Connie said she hadn't heard from him, but made a prescient guess: *If he did he probably (inaudible) his truck by now. Ray was a police officer and he wouldn't want to go to jail . . . what's the word?*

Bob answered, but the word is marked inaudible. Only snippets of the final pages are preserved. The transcript ends with a series of questions, the answers to which are lost forever. The transcript is the only surviving record of that conversation. The tape has been destroyed. Bob's dead. Connie left town, and even if I found her, she probably wouldn't remember. There's no way to recover exactly what was said, no way of knowing.

The interview began just after Connie called my brother, just after I stood on the porch of our house in Tucson and watched him hang up the phone, and only now do I remember what I was doing while the detectives were asking these questions: walking from room to room in the house where I last saw her, picking things up and putting them down, thinking there must be an answer somewhere if only I could find it.

All these years later, I'm still doing the same thing.

Wyatt Earp died the morning of January 13, 1929, in a one-room apartment in Los Angeles. The man a bullet never touched died quietly, at eighty, of a prostate condition. Wyatt had outlived all five of his brothers and two wives, and he had no children. He'd lost most of his money during decades of gambling and bad investments, was living off of charity, and years of reading lies about his life had made him bitter. But his biographer claimed Wyatt was optimistic to the end, still planning another trip out to the desert. As he died in that cheap apartment, delusional and broke, I doubt anyone said of Wyatt Earp that he'd made the wrong choices in life.

He'd ridden out of Tombstone fifty years earlier, but he could never live it down. Wyatt said he hoped he'd fade into obscurity after he died, that he'd finally be left alone. But he told that to a biographer whose tall tales of Wyatt's life would cement his legend.

Wyatt claimed to have no regrets about the Gunfight at the O.K. Corral and its aftermath, except that those few months defined his life. He didn't mention the three men killed in the fight, nor his own brother Morgan, murdered in revenge. He said that if he had the gunfight to do over, he would have done exactly what he did.

But his last words were an unfinished question: *Suppose, suppose . . .*

The last person to see my mother alive was a former neighbor, Mrs. Miller, who owned a ranch outside of Tombstone. The final pages of the police report are a deputy's interview of her. Mrs. Miller said she saw my mother and Ray on Wednesday morning. She was driving toward Tombstone and they were headed out, Ray at the wheel, one arm out the window. She waved. He waved back.

The deputy interviewing her asked if my mother and Ray were heading toward Gleeson. Mrs. Miller said they could have been. He asked if there was anybody else in the truck and she said no. He asked when Mrs. Miller had last been to my mother's house and she said never, but that she'd known my mother for many years. She mentioned some of the businesses my mother had owned, and that she had dated several different men.

The deputy asked if they appeared to be having any problems when she saw them. Mrs. Miller said no, they were just driving slowly up the road, like they always did. She saw them often, on the road or in the post office or at the Walmart in Sierra Vista, and they'd be holding hands and sticking close together. She didn't know them to ever have had problems— they were always kissing and hugging when she saw them— but on that Wednesday she did wonder to herself if they were still as lovey as they'd always been. She didn't say what gave her that impression, and the deputy didn't ask.

Mrs. Miller said she saw them at about nine-fifteen. Bob found her body between three and three-thirty, already cold. When Mrs. Miller saw my mother, she had a few hours left to live, and was leaving Tombstone for the last time, being driven slowly out into the desert.

The road on the left hugs a barbed-wire fence for about a quarter mile until it comes to a rusted gate hanging open. My memory sparks but doesn't catch until I imagine that gate closed, and remember my mother standing by the gatepost, twisting the combination lock, swinging it open, turning, smiling, waving me through. She kept the gate closed. The police report says it was open the day they found her. The last time I was here, I removed the police tape and opened it again. Whoever lives here now leaves it open; they must feel safer than she did.

Past the gate the road dips sharply, crosses an arroyo, rises again. My car won't make it any farther, but it doesn't have to. It's coming back to me now. Ahead, that side track to the left must have been the turnoff to their driveway. After I left the trailer, I walked down to that wash and stared at her blood on my hands. She died halfway up that hill.

I don't know what I expected, if I thought I'd come here and replay that day eight years ago, walk into the trailer, stare off down the valley again, wondering what had happened. But there's no reason to get out of the car, nowhere to go, nothing to see. Everything I remember is gone. No trailer, no corrals, no red sign saying "WHOA." A square shape on the horizon might be a small building, a shed, but it's too far away to have been hers; otherwise it's a bare hillside, just another patch of land parceled off by a barbed-wire fence.

Maybe I have the wrong place; maybe I can't even remember where she died. Or maybe the new owners removed the reminders of the murder that happened here, and who can blame them? We sold it for a song, didn't want to be reminded. Now I show up all these years later and it's not what I expected. What did I expect? A diorama showing where they stood and shot and died, like the one at the O.K. Corral? Coming here was a bad idea. Now I'm just another tourist.

My vision blurs. My hands begin to shake. A burn spreads through my chest. Whatever closure I was hoping to find here is never going to come, only more of this same old rage. Since she died, it's like I'm trapped in a house on fire.

I turn the car around and drive back toward the main road, breathing deeply, trying to calm down. A blue sedan turns in ahead of me and pulls over to let me pass. I stop next to it and roll my window down. Inside, an old white couple watches me like a threat; these might be the new owners of my mother's land, the people who erased all sign of her. The man's large balding head turns to the woman, and his jowls shake as he speaks. Her glasses cover her entire face, reflecting a warped view of the desert. He pushes a button and his window falls.

"Is this your land?" I say it loud, and he recoils. I'll buy it back, right here and now, no matter what it costs. I'll build that rammed-earth house with my bare hands, make her a monument.

The stranger shakes his head and gives a sheepish smile, a little shrug. "Nope," he says. "We're just looking for the ghost town."

She would have been facing west. It was warm that day, ninety at noon; the windows of the trailer were open, and through them she saw the mottled hills, tawny and green, rising and falling into the distance; the horses ambling in the corral, muscles bunching beneath their sleek hides as they moved; the charred ring where the fire pit had been. Outside, the door of the truck slammed shut. She returned to her crossword puzzle, reread the clue. What was the word?

The trailer door opened. A shaft of light, a breath of wind, a boot thumping on the step. She ignored him. They had fought about something, said things that couldn't be unsaid. She tried to forget about it, to focus on the clue. She wasn't one to brood. If she had made a decision, to leave that place, to leave Ray, she wouldn't have wavered. She knew how to make decisions.

He said something or he didn't. She replied or she didn't. I hope he hesitated before he raised my mother's gun and pointed it at her back, hope it was hard for him to become that man. If she sensed what was coming, she didn't turn around.

A tug at her shoulder. A crack split the room. Another. The pain arrived an instant later, in her shoulder, in her chest, spreading, ricocheting. She had known pain, but this was fresh and terrible. *Pain* was just a word.

She slumped against the shelf. The book fell to the floor. Her world went slow. The word, she had just thought of it, and now it was gone, the puzzle left unsolved. He must have said something then, but I doubt she grasped his words. She must have felt what I do, words failing. Once she'd known what love meant, had said the word in vows, and she'd used it again and again, meaning something different every time, until it brought her here, to a place without a name, with a man she didn't love anymore, and now the words were done. Only acts remained. She was going to die.

His bootheels beat on the floor as he approached. She whirled and raked her nails across his face. He shoved her away. She landed facedown on the shelf and knew that he was aiming. She never would have thought he'd shoot her in the back.

In that last moment she must have felt it all acutely. Pain. The sun on her back. The tang of gunpowder on her tongue. A shred of desert through the window. The last swell of hope: if she could talk him down, it was only her shoulder, she could call an ambulance, she might still live. She clenched a hand against her wound, loved her body for doing what it was told, loved it more now that it wasn't hers for long. She must have thought of her parents, her brother, her horses. God.

And her children. Where we were. How we'd hear. What we'd do without her, the men we would become. Her hopes for us, the weddings and grandkids she would miss. The bond we had. Reading to us in the womb before we knew the words. The messages she'd sent us from the sky when she'd thought the end was near. As a shadow arm rose on the wall, as she braced for the bullet, she would have tried to speak to her sons. We might not hear her now. We might not think we could. But she believed that one day we would hear her voice again, and know that she had never left us.

AUTHOR'S NOTE

T he events depicted in this book happened, and the people exist. When possible, sources other than memory have been used to verify facts, including journal entries, letters and emails, photographs, videotapes, police reports, newspaper and magazine articles, recordings and transcripts of personal interviews, and my own notes. Some names, including company names, potentially identifying details and locations, have been changed to disguise the individuals involved. Some events are presented outside of their actual chronology. Some of the dialogue is reconstructed from my memory of conversations; some is selected, excerpted, and edited from interview recordings and transcripts; some is included verbatim.

Historical information about Tombstone, the Earps, and the events surrounding the Gunfight at the O.K. Corral comes from many different sources. Many of the facts of Tombstone's history are matters of dispute, and in those cases I chose whatever version I found most compelling. Casey Tefertiller's excellent biography, *Wyatt Earp: The Life Behind the Legend*, was especially useful in the researching and writing of this book. The following sources were also consulted:

After the Boom in Tombstone and Jerome, Arizona: Decline in Western Resource Towns, by Eric L. Clements

And Die in the West: The Story of the O.K. Corral Gunfight, by Paula Mitchell Marks

Helldorado: Bringing the Law to the Mesquite, by William M. Breakenridge

The Private Journal of George Whitwell Parsons, edited by Lynn R. Bailey

Tombstone (book), by Walter Noble Burns

Tombstone (movie), written by Kevin Jarre

Too Tough to Die: The Rise, Fall, and Resurrection of a Silver Camp, 1878 to 1990, by Lynn R. Bailey

Wyatt Earp: Frontier Marshal, by Stuart N. Lake

ACKNOWLEDGMENTS

This book took a long time, and a lot of people helped along the way. I'd like to thank my agent, Julie Barer, for always being there, and for always being right; Noah Eaker, my editor, for his diligence and care in making this book better; Margo Rabb, for being its first reader and champion; Laura Ford, for believing in this project from the beginning; Judy Clain, for her gracious and selfless advice; everyone at Random House; and everybody at Barer Literary, especially William Boggess, Leah Heifferon, and Anna Weiner.

I'm especially grateful to the friends and colleagues whose advice and feedback helped me at critical points in the process: Andrew Foster Altschul, Molly Antopol, Bonnie Arning, Will Boast, Harriet Clark, Rob Ehle, Stephen Elliott, John Evans, Sarah Frisch, Jim Gavin, Skip Horack, Vanessa Hutchinson, Ammi Keller, Josh Rivkin, Mike Scalise, Stephanie Soileau, Chanan Tigay, JM Tyree, Abigail Ulman, and Jesmyn Ward. I would also like to thank my teachers, especially Robert Hous-

---

ton, for his encouragement, and Tobias Wolff, for his advice and his example. The Stanford Creative Writing Program supported me during the writing of this book, and I'm honored to have been a part of that remarkable community of writers and teachers. I'd also like to thank the University of Arizona's English and creative writing faculty for teaching me how to write.

Thanks to the men and women of the Cochise County Sheriff's Office for their work on my mother's case, and for their help in researching this book. Thanks to everyone who appears in these pages, by their real names or otherwise. Special thanks to Parents of Murdered Children and the people I met there—as well as to Connie Juel, another survivor—for reminding me that our stories matter. I'd also like to acknowledge the complete lack of cooperation of KVOA Channel 4 in Tucson and the Tombstone Marshal's Department.

For being there when we needed them most, thanks to Peter Bidegain, Joe Huntsman, Orion McKotter, Stacy Mitchell, and Nolana Nerhan. Other friends have helped and inspired me in more ways than they knew: Charlie Bertsch, Connor Doyle, Mike and Anna Doyle, Ryan and Kim Finley and the Finley family, D. Seth Horton, Ric Jahna, Christa Mussi, and Jim Wheeler. Love and thanks to the Reischl family—Julie, Robert, Marques, and Byron—as well as the Moncayo, Chirco, and Nurss families, who, together, have never let me feel alone. Love and gratitude to Laura "Tennessee" McKee, for her patience and grace.

Most of all, I'd like to thank my family: my brother, Josh; my grandmother; my cousins, Leighanne and Sean and Eric; my grandfather, John Bennis, the best man I ever knew; and my mother, Deborah Ann Bennis, for raising me, and for all the sacrifices.

ABOUT THE AUTHOR

Justin St. Germain was born in Philadelphia in 1981. He attended the University of Arizona and was a Wallace Stegner Fellow at Stanford. He lives in Albuquerque.